Religiosity in African Christian Churches

Tresphor C. Mutale

Langaa Research & Publishing CIG
Mankon, Bamenda

Publisher:
Langaa RPCIG
Langaa Research & Publishing Common Initiative Group
P.O. Box 902 Mankon
Bamenda
North West Region
Cameroon
Langaagrp@gmail.com
www.langaa-rpcig.net

Distributed in and outside N. America by African Books Collective
orders@africanbookscollective.com
www.africanbookscollective.com

ISBN-10: 9956-552-42-9

ISBN-13: 978-9956-552-42-9

© Tresphor C. Mutale 2022

All rights reserved.
No part of this book may be reproduced or transmitted in any form or by any means, mechanical or electronic, including photocopying and recording, or be stored in any information storage or retrieval system, without written permission from the publisher

Dedication

Augustine Chifulo Mutale and Marian Bwalya Mutale
With a lot of affection and gratitude

Acknowledgement

This book is an off-shoot of valuable contributions from different people of different backgrounds. Among the contributors to the realization of this humble book are, Prof. Chammah Kaunda – Yonsei University - South Korea, Nelly Mwale Chita - University of Zambia, Peter Kayula (PHD), Mauricio .B. Chileshe, Idol Nkandu - Kesaria Seminary in Zambia and several others for their useful criticisms, suggestions and raising further questions.

Table of Contents

Acknowledgements: v

Glossary and Terminology: ix

Foreword: xiii
Chammah J. Kaunda

Author's Preface: xix

Introduction: 1

Chapter 1: Anthropological Context of African Life 9
1.1. Differentiations among African Cultures........................... 16
1.2. Colonization through Religion.. 32
1.3. The Concept of Religion in Africa...................................... 41
1.4. Religion as a Peculiar Phenomenon................................... 45
1.5. Interaction between Religion and Politics in Zambia 51
1.6. Spiritual Power of Interconnectedness............................... 56
1.7. Under the Physical Reality.. 60
1.8. Science and African Traditional Religions 64

Chapter 2: Myths and Socio-Cultural Experiences in Zambia.. 71
2.1. Supernatural Myths in Zambia 74
2.2. Witchcraft and Magical Myths 76
2.2.1. Bronislaw Malinowski on Mystical Beliefs..................... 77
2.2.2. Sigmund Freud on Mystical Beliefs 81
2.2.3. Edward Burnett Tylor on Mystical Beliefs 83
2.3. Belief in Witchcraft and Traditional Magic in Zambia...... 86

Chapter 3: Reality and Existence of Evil in African Traditional Religions 93
3.1. God as the cause of Evil.. 95
3.2. Spirits of the Dead as the cause of Evil 98
3.3. The Living as the cause of Evil 100

Chapter 4: Ritual- Power in African Traditional Religions ... 103
4.1. Power and Authority of the Ritual Leaders ... 107
4.2. Ritual Leaders as Intermediaries ... 107
4.3. Mediumistic Role of Ritual Leaders ... 108
4.4. Nature and importance of African Ritual ... 110

Chapter 5: Religious Groups and African Life ... 125
5.1. Fragmentation of Religions in African ... 125
5.2. Ritual leadership in African Traditional Religions ... 126
5.3. Christian Fundamentalism and African Tradition Religions ... 130
5.4. Doctrine and African Traditional Belief Systems ... 134
5.5. Syncretism as a Euro-Christian Conflict ... 141

Chapter 6: Domestication of Christian Symbols ... 147
6.1. Anointing Oils, Holy Water and Christian Instruments ... 149
6.2. Priests, Pastors, Apostles, Prophets and Men of God ... 152
6.3. Religious Predation in Africa ... 154
6.4. Control of Predation in Religion in Africa ... 158

Conclusion ... 165

Bibliography ... 169

Glossary and Terminology

Babemba. This is one of the biggest tribes in Zambia. The Babemba are originally from Luba – Lunda Empire in the Congo who came and settled in the Northern part of Zambia during the early migration period that occurred in Central Africa in the eighteenth century.

Chansa. It means "that which/who covers". This is also a Bemba philosophical attribute of God from the manner in which God has spread out creation in its wonder. It is an expression of wonder about creativity in which God has covered the earth with nature. It is a common local name for people among the Babemba people.

Imfwa yakwa Lesa. It is a Bemba reference to death that is interpreted to find its origin in the desire and plan of God.

Ishamo. In ciBemba it means "a curse".

Kamunyama/Bakamunyama. A general term referring to a ritual killer(s) who kill human beings for body parts for use in magic or for trafficking purposes among Zambians.

Ku-solola. It is Ndembu (one of the tribes in the North Western province of Zambia) symbolic term or expression, meaning "to make Visible" or "to reveal" what is hidden.

Lesa. Name of God in ciBemba language.

Lesa ni malyotola, ala lyotola. It is a Bemba expression about the power of God to punish those who abrogate his norms with impunity.

Lumpa Church. This is a Christian church established by a woman, "Alice Lenshina Mulenga" in Kasama of Northern Rhodesia in 1953. The church believed in the blending and promotion of Christian and African traditional religious beliefs and practices against the teaching of traditional Christian churches.

Mulenga. It is a Bemba attribute of God in cibemba language. It means, an "artist". It is an attribute referred to God because of the marvellous art seen in what God has created. God is perceived as a great artist. Mulenga in Zambia is a common name for people among the BaBemba.

Mulungu. It is one of the names of God in a number of local languages in Zambia and outside Zambia.

Ntumbanambo mutima kayebele. This is a Bemba expression among the attributes of God as one who cannot be influenced in his plans, desires, decisions and judgments in anyway. He does things from his own desires. Meaning that God is self-willed.

Nyami Nyami. This is a Tonga name for a local god. This is known as the "Zambezi River God" or "Zambezi snake spirit". It is believed to be one of the most important male gods of the Tonga people of southern Zambia.

Shicaibumba. This is another attribute of God in icibemba language. This literary means "self – created". It is a reference to who God is.

Ubwanga. It can refer to the paraphernalia of witchcraft. It includes all what is used in witchcraft.

Ukubalishamo. This is a popular street expression among Zambians which literary means, "to feed others or someone" or "to get a part or a cut". This now has come to mean sharing the spoils of corruption or fraud or getting a cut from a deal.

Ukuswamo. This is another popular street expression which literary means, "picking something from a garden or a field". A state today in Zambia is seen as a garden or a field where one can pick or harvest personal wealth using under hand methods.

Mzimu or Munda. A spirit in Kiswahili

D.R.C. Democratic Republic of Congo (Former Zaire)

E.S.A.P. Economic Structural Adjustment Programme

I.M.F. International Monetary Fund

N.D.F. National Dialogue Forum

B.W.A.C. Berlin West-Africa Conference

H.I.V. Human Immunodeficiency Virus

Covid 19. Coronavirus Disease 19

A.I.C. African Instituted (Independent) Churches

Foreword

Of 'Religious Schizophrenics' and 'Strangers Within': Making Sense of Irrationalities in African Christianity

The state of Christianity in Africa today exhibits what could be described as 'the split[1] narcissist religious imaginations' (Sigmund Freud's "split ego" and Jacques Lacan's 'split subjectivity'). This is essentially a dissociated or fractured religious consciousness located between the inferior-self wrought by colonial racialization and the quest for postcolonial emancipated imaginary-self which are alternately dominant in the practices and expressions of Christianity.

It is a suspension in the twilight zones between being classical Western Christianity and African traditional religions that describes the intersections between the almost known and almost unknown religious self. It is the distortion or alteration of ability to distinguish between the sacred and profane, between good and evil or between God and the Devil.

This, in turn, has given rise to a paradox of religious subjectivities (Edmund Husserl) which could be interpreted as a suspended religious consciousness of Africans as the most disgraced-brutalized-dehumanized-self and the post-colonial emancipated imaginary-self in the mirror as fully human and master of own destiny (Frantz Fanon). The only problem is that 'the destiny' is they pursue a shadow representation of Western idea - that which modern global coloniality has already defined and determined for Africans. This pursuit of illusory reality and not knowing that it is just illusions has created what the late Ghanaian Christian scholar Kwame Bediako defines as a "lingering dilemma of an Africa uncertain of its identity".

---

1 Nimi Wariboko has used the theory of split to describe a theoretical possibility of Nigerian Pentecostals understanding of God. See his, The Split God: Pentecostalism and Critical Theory (Albany, New York: State University of New York Press, 2018).

² An African experience of religion as a dark void in which the self is permanently trapped and subjected to perpetually reliving itself alternatively as a pseudo-Western and as the wretched of the earth[3], sometimes both and sometimes as none. Mutua Makau describes this phenomenon as a 'religio-cultural suspension between a blurred African past and a distorted Westernized existence.'[4]

African Christian (especially, Pentecostal) beliefs and practices might have appearance of Western Christianity and African traditional religions, but at a deeper observation, it becomes clear that they are neither African nor Western but located within borderline of African and Western religious consciousness. South African Archbishop Desmond Tutu names this experience as 'religious schizophrenia',[5] the Kenyan theologian, Joseph Galgalo classifies it as 'living with the stranger within'[6] – a dissociative identity.

The interaction between Africanity and Christianity have not resulted in the formation of a unified idea of religion, rather has sanctioned rituals and healing practices that make African religious experience as in a split narcissist way as a fractured self within. This has been reinforced by the fact that most Africans continue to perceive themselves as subjects in an objectifying and racializing global society in which to express and practice religion is itself an act of struggle for emancipation, especially from economic underdevelopment.

Economic development is important here because it appears to be a key defining and determining factors of who is fully human and who is less human. Economic underdevelopment suggests that Africans are not fully human. This collective stress of seeking to authenticate the full humanity of Africans has also contributed to the

---

2 Kwame Bediako, Christianity in Africa: The Renewal of a Non-Western Religion (Edinburgh: Edinburgh University Press, and Maryknoll, N.Y.: Orbis, 1995), 5.

3 Frantz Fanon, The Wretched of the Earth, Transl. Constance Farrington (New York: Grove Press, 1963).

4 Mutua, Makau, Human Rights: A Political and Cultural Critique (Philadelphia: University of Pennsylvania Press, 2002), 66.

5 Desmond M. Tutu, "Black Theology/African Theology - Soul Mates or Antagonists?" A Reader in African Christian Theology edited by John Parratt (London: SPCK, 1987), 36-44.

6 Joseph D. Galgalo, African Christianity: The stranger within (Lumuru: Zapf Chancery Publishers Africa, 2012), 15.

creation of postcolonial 'split narcissist religious imaginations' in African Christianity.

It appears the only thing that Africans have that has some value is religion. This stereo typical representation of Africa and Africans has been validated by some African scholars such as John Samuel Mbiti who argued that "Africans are notoriously religious"[7] and reinforced by some Africanists who name Africa as "the world's most religious continent".[8] African pursuit of religious ideas might not be different from other human races, what appears to be distinctive is the way Africans understand the role of religion in their world.

Religion in Africa is not necessarily about the search for the world to come, rather a source of hope, of inspiration, to escape or negotiate the dominant realities and the means to be reborn into a world of abundant life for all (or in the post-colonial times, to be reborn into a world devoid of economic disgrace).

Thus, religion is perceived as an enchanted gateway arch holding a promise of new opportunities for experiencing the postcolonial emancipated imagery self in the mirror within the constantly shifting order of modern global coloniality. However, as Tresphor Mutale demonstrates, the search for this postcolonial emancipated imagery self has come at a great cost. It has engendered 'the split narcissist forms of religious expressions' or what Tresphor Mutale classifies as "irrationalities" which include sexually molesting and raping women and children, murder, human trafficking, instructing single women to attend worship without underwear; sucking single women's breasts as a way of exorcising demons out of them; claiming to be instructed by the Holy Spirit to have sexual intercourse with married women simultaneously with their daughters; spraying pesticides such as doom on their congregants as a healing therapy for HIV and cancer; excessively wealthy and wildly extravagant lifestyle among pastors; selling religious objects and prayers for miracles etc.[9] It is like religion gone haywire or its ministers have gone rogue. This 'mafialization' of religion is not only inherently shocking but raises some serious

---

[7] John, Samuel, Mbiti, African Religions and Philosophy (London, Ibadan, Nairobi: Heinemann, 1969).

[8] Jenny, Trinitapoli and Alexander Weinreb, Religion and AIDS in Africa (New York: Oxford University Press, 2012).

[9] Chammah J. Kaunda, "The Emptied Authority': African Neo-Pentecostalism, Modernisation Of Sacred Authority, And Gendered and Sexualised Constructions Of Violence," *Acta Theologica* 40, no. 2 (2020): 216-237.

concerns about the nature and the future of Christianity in the continent.

Scholars from a parade of disciplines have sought the concepts to understand, explain and articulate the source of irrationalities in Christianity in Africa. Tresphor Mutale helps us to understand that only through interrogating how African traditional religions are inculturated can we adequately comprehend such split narcissist expressions and practices of African Christianity. African traditional religions have not only influenced Christianity but remain resilient and a force behind the massive presence of Christianity in Africa.

The fundamental elements of African traditional religions such as the quest for abundant life, no permanent and precise members, ritual rather than dogmatic oriented, spiritual powers etc. have found new expressions in Christianity. Christianity was introduced within the Western culture of the individualism which also shaped capitalism. The culture of individualism is a foundational character of Western capitalism. It appears that individualism and capitalism have found fertile ground in some key elements of African traditional religions such as those aforementioned. For example, the quest for abundant life has been translated into prosperity gospel with its capitalist orientation; resistance to permanent members has promoted individualism and fragmentation of Christianity, and traditional prioritization of the ritual over dogmatics nurtures and nourishes the dominant expressions and practices of Christianity in Africa.

It appears that there has been an organic inculturation or domestication of Christian symbols through ascribing them with mystical powers of traditional religions to attract and scam a mass of mystified Africans.[10] This domestication has come as a result of collective trauma and stress of colonization and postcolonial search to 'catch-up' with Western economic development and prove that Africans are as authentic and fully human as white Euro-Americans. This is not in any way justifying rogue Christianity, rather suggest that psychoanalysis approaches could be a useful tool for interrogating and making sense of the borderline expressions defining African Christianity. This does not in any way negate the Africanness of Christianity as the book demonstrates, Christianity with its various

---

[10] Chammah J. Kaunda, 'The Nation That Fears God Prospers': A Critique of Zambian Pentecostal Theopolitical Imaginations (Philadelphia: Fortress, 2018).

challenges and in diverse manifestations has become truly African religion. However, it might require psychotherapy!

Chammah J. Kaunda
The United Graduate School of Theology,
Yonsei University, Seoul, South Korea
January 8, 2022

Author's Preface

This book has been provoked by what is being experienced in the area of religion in many parts of Africa; particularly in the many parts of Zambia. Religion today on many occasions is defying reason or rationality and scientific technological applications and knowledge. Religion seems to be raising some fundamental questions in regard to some spiritual experiences being attested to. An African religious sense seems not to differentiate irrationality from what is rational when it comes to religion from a western philosophical point of view.

The scientific and technological worlds that surround an African appear not to inform an African about some fundamental reality. The religious aspect of African life overrides nearly every other aspect of African life.

At the same time the authority of an African religious leader appears to have some power of influence that is difficult to understand and to grasp. In some cases, the authority of a religious leader is more compelling than that of a lawyer, a politician, a scientist, a medical doctor and other known traditional authorities, which is in contrast to the western mind.

One would argue that authority and power of an African religious leader at the moment appear not to be contested and questioned because it is authority taken for granted – authority that goes without saying. It is power considered to come from above shrouded in mystics and sacredness.

Therefore, this authority is likely to defy reason, science and technological power. Today, it is however, a fact from some reports and testimonies that religion in some cases has the power to subjugate and make followers submissive to some irrational and inhuman acts. People who have been victims of this power and authority sometimes justify the actions done or carried on them by the men of God on the basis of faith and belief.

Were an objective person, outside the context of religious experience will conclude to have seen some outright abuse, fraud, manipulation, exploitation instead, the victim experiences the work and power of the hand of God at play.

God is attributed as the main protagonist in these sometimes, irrational and exploitative, manipulative and abusive experiences. It should not be forgotten easily that history of religion attests to the fact that religion has generally played both positive and negative roles in human society.

From a positive point of view, religion has united people of different backgrounds, nationalities and ethnicities, rich and poor together based on belief and it has fought injustices and inequalities among humanity. However, history is not blind to some irrational, horrors and atrocities committed in the name of religion and in the name of faith.

Terrorism, slavery, divisions and violence in the name of religion are some of the negatives religion has perpetrated and found itself in. For example, the bitter historical relationships between the Arabs and Jews in the Middle East, Christians and Moslems in some Sub-Saharan African, Indonesia, Middle East and Hindus and Moslems in East Asia.

Religion in some cases has been found wanting in the areas of abuse and manipulation of vulnerable members of society especially children and women. In some cases, issues of maladministration by religious authorities of resources contributed by members in the name of faith have been reported and brought to light.

Some religious leaders who have been at the centre of these abuses have not been compelled to account because they willed a lot of religious power and authority. All these have been wrapped up in extraordinary authority and power of an African religious leader.

Today, how do we explain a situation of a male pastor requesting to anoint the sexual body parts of a female member of a congregation in order to conceive? Or some pastor engaging in what may be called "ritual sexual intercourse" with a member of a congregation in order to conceive in the name of religious belief? What makes people to fall in these fraudulent and irrational religious traps? Why are some African Christian religious leaders approaching religion as if they are African traditional healers, diviners and witch-finders? This book makes a critical interpretation of these "irrational" experiences through the eyes of African traditional religions. African traditional religions in this case provide instruments for interpreting the current religious scenario.

This book tries to make a critique from the point of view of African religious cultural tradition in the context of African Christian Churches to give an explanation to some fundamental questions being raised about some of the spiritual experiences today.

This book is not justifying the religious abuses, frauds and manipulations as being part of African traditional religions. The book tries to pull out and explicate rationality out of what may be seen as irrational by an outsider.

It looks at how African traditional religions have influenced Christian beliefs in some fundamental ways. The book looks at the power of the symbolisms of African traditional religions and how these have been interpreted in the context of new religion of Christianity.

The book shows how African traditional beliefs have been weaved neatly in Christian traditions and expressions. At the same time, the book grapples with what lies behind what can be perceived by general sense as irrational in African's religious experiences. The methods that inform this book are based on documentary and the author's experiences. These include what has been documented by academicians, media reports and other sources of information.

Tresphor Mutale
Masaiti, Zambia
October 7, 2021

Introduction

> "... a man's own experience of belief cannot be taken from him merely because others disbelieve. His obscure, inarticulable experience of God may have meaning only for him ...so much so that it outweighs all challenges brought against it".[1]

In recent years we have experienced some marked spiritual and religious experiences in Christianity in Africa in general and Zambia in particular which have raised some questions. These spiritual experiences have been punctuated by prophecies, miracles, spiritual testimonies, healing and not forgetting to mention the proliferation of independent Christian churches. It appears that today in Zambia we have more Christian churches than secondary schools, clinics and development co-operatives. Some of the public places like bars and social clubs which were under the local authorities before 1991 economic liberalization in Zambia have been turned into churches. It is not long ago that the government of the Republic of Zambia, through the Ministry of Education, put a stop to some churches using schools for prayers and worship. This was so common that nearly every school was used as a place of prayer and worship on the weekends.

Some schools would have more than two different denominations every Sunday. In some of these churches, congregants would testify to some religious experiences in terms of healing, prophecy, miracles and other mystical religious experiences. To accommodate proliferation of churches the Local Authorities designate some special pieces of land for churches. In these areas you would find sometimes more than three different churches with different approaches to Christianity.

These spiritual experiences have been a challenge to the "traditional churches" and to socio-political governance of African societies to an extent that there is today some strong voice that advocates control of religious institutions through legal means.

---

[1] Michael Novak, Belief and Unbelief: A Philosophy of Self-knowledge (New York and Toronto: The New American Library, 1965), 20.

There is a call to monitor the level of qualifications in theology for someone to be considered a pastor of a religious institution. This is due to Christianity which has become so segmented and polarized. This practical aspect of Christianity may be termed as the "relativization of expression of Christianity". There are now different approaches to evangelization and spiritual care for the souls of people. Markets, buses, schools, shopping malls, bus stations and street corners have become spaces for evangelization.

At some level Christianity has become an industry on its own which is generating millions and millions of dollars or an economic capital based on its liberalization. In Zambia proliferation of independent Christian, prophetic and Charismatic churches came at the same time when the economy was being liberalized in the early 1990s after shifting away from One Party State dispensation. Therefore, it was not only the liberalization of the economy through democratic dispensation; partly it was and indirectly included the liberalization in the expression of Christianity as well.

It will be interesting to study and investigate how much money is being generated by these churches, especially in Africa annually. We are seeing a shift in Christianity from emphasis on "being" to "having". The "Gospel of prosperity" has taken a centre stage. Pastors and men of God have become symbols of what it means to have faith and believe in God by their prosperous and luxurious lives.

The sense of eschatological aspect has slowly been replaced by life in the now. Even in the traditional Churches we are seeing more emphasis on "mammon" than salvation of souls. Some of the wealthiest people we have in the world and Africa in particular are the church leaders, Bishops, Pastors, Seers, Prophets or simply "men of God".

Their wealth and luxurious lifestyles of big cars, planes, exquisite houses, investments, are believed to set as a model of faith in God. It is believed that they are wealthy because they have strong belief and faith in God. Faith and wealth have become synonymous. Faith in God generates physical wealth and well - being of a true believer.

The field of religion has been opened to different expressions of prayers, teachings and approaches to the divine. We are witnessing a proliferation African instituted or independent Churches. Some of these have broken away from the historical churches or main line churches.

The independent churches include spiritual or Pentecostal churches which offer a range of ways that enhance emotional aspects of human life. Some are called prophetic churches because they are built on a prophet. Some are known as Apostolic churches because they have apostles in their expression of authority.

They are known as African Instituted Churches (AIC) for they are founded on and led by Africans. Some of these churches may not be exclusively described based on only one of the above. They may encompass more than one description. What is true is the fact that they represent a cultural renaissance as partly a reaction to the mission of the historical or main line churches.[2]

Today we have Christian mega churches, "synagogues", cathedrals, ministries, mountains and chapels as symbols of Christian institutions. These numerous religious institutions have given people freedom to choose their spiritual identity. At the same time, it has given people freedom even to travel thousands of kilometres to meet the "true men of God".

These same "men of God" are free to go out to preach the word of God anywhere and in any country for the salvation of the people. These expressions of Christian religion and freedoms have raised many questions than answers. Some men of God have come into conflict with the laws of the host countries where they travel to conduct their Godly given gifts and deported. Some have even been on wanted list by some governments for fraud and money laundering.[3]

There is now some rise in different expressions of Christianity through prophetic, charismatic, healers and independent churches. Some spiritual experiences being testified to seem to border on manipulation, abuse, aggression, violence and fraud from an outsider.

Religion in Africa and elsewhere has become a lucrative business and investment. Religion is interwoven with and accommodated into capitalism to a greater extent. In the context of capitalism there has developed today what is popularly known as "Christianity of prosperity". This is a type of Christianity that preaches physical

---

[2] John S., Pobee, "African Instituted (Independent) Churches", Dictionary of the Ecumenical Movement, ed. Nicholas, Lossky et all (Geneva: William B. Eerdmans Publishing Company, Grand Rapids, 1991), 10 – 11.

[3] www.timeslive.co.za, Bushiri Mansion will be auctioned after being forfeited to State: NPA; globalpressjournal.com, Zambia begins crackdown on Self-proclaimed Prophets. Accessed on 17.03.2021.

prosperity and wealth creation in the life of the followers by giving more to God and getting blessed in return.

Critical thinking has come to inform many people today, that actually, it is wealth creation for the "men of God". However, many still believe in the connection between physical wealth and faith in God.

The above is true because Christianity today especially in Africa and Zambia in particular is registering more abuses, in form of sexual and financial mismanagement, political manipulations and fraud. To this extent some African countries are calling for civil legal framework on the operations of the churches to make the churches accountable not only to God but to the followers and the society as well.[4]

This has already been strongly echoed by President Paul Kagame and his country Rwanda calling for a new legislation to have control on the operations of the churches with regard to minimum academic qualifications (theological studies) for church leaders and conditions in which the churches operate. Kigali alone was reported to have about 700 churches which shocked the president of Rwanda, Paul Kagame.

The government of Rwanda after this concern closed to over 6 000 churches across the country.[5] The blame here is partly put squarely on the pastors of churches as not being well schooled and prepared to evangelize in rational ways. It is argued that lack of well-schooled and theologically informed, formed and sound pastors turn to be abusive to the people they lead. It can however be argued that the challenge is much more than lack of sound theological schooling of some religious leaders.

Some of the actions of these men of God are out-right abuses and manipulations. The question to be asked is why do their followers fall in the trap of abuse and manipulation? These calls are emanating from the reported abuses being experienced today, ranging from sexual misconducts, both aggressive and passive violence, financial

---

[4] bbc.com, Why some African governments are clamping down on churches. Accessed on 19.02.2021; pmg.org.za, Commercialization of Religion and Abuse of people's belief system. Accessed on 17.03.2021.

[5] news24.com, Rwanda closes thousands of churches in a bid for more control; bbc.com, Rwanda church closures: Pastors arrested for defying order. Accessed on 19.02.2021.

fraud and other considerations of "irrationality" perpetrated by church leaderships or men of God.

It can be argued that the challenge is not with the church leaders only. For many of these men of God are well educated, schooled and they use their education to manipulate and abuse the people. They use the word of God they have learnt and studied to wood-wink or manipulate the people into submission, subjugation and irrationality.

Therefore, the challenge is more than inadequate theological education of the "men of God" but the cultural setup of African society in relation to religious beliefs and systems which drives people into being manipulated and abused.

In the context of this religious and spiritual change taking place, this book labours to explain these spiritual experiences and religiosity from the nature of African traditional religions' point of view. It is a contribution to answer, why many Africans are falling prey to these manipulations and fraudulent abuses in the name of spiritual experiences.

The book tries to see some "rationality" in the "irrational". The question is, why is it that the victims of some religious experiences are not able to see the irrationality of certain spiritual experiences? The simple answer is that these irrational experiences are veiled and packaged in the logic of cultural practices and beliefs – world view. Cultural logic and beliefs are corrupted by and through the spiritual authority of the religious leaders for personal wealth creation through irrational and fraudulent spiritual experiences.

The work in this book argues that these spiritual experiences in Africa today are not new in essence. In them there is something that is at the core of African traditional religions that is being expressed in a totally new capitalistic and individualistic environment. It can be interpreted as an expression of African traditional religions in a modern society, using modern and capitalistic symbolisms.

This work is a contribution to understanding, interpreting the spiritual and religious expressions and experiences as we have them today. Actually, this work does not provide anything new about African way of life. It only provides and interprets new ways of expressing African belief systems in the capitalistic environment.

This book is based on theoretical and practical expression of African traditional religions. It points to the dynamic nature of African traditional religions in its practical expression. It puts to the test the theory that African traditional religions are not dynamic by some academic arguments. The book applies the logic of African traditional religions and applied in the present, modern capitalistic, pluralistic and liberalized society.

This book appears to be more open-ended, but being fully aware that it cannot accommodate the African spiritual experiences and religious life in their totality. This is so because African spirituality and religions are not aspects standing on their own like in the Western Christian religion. Religion in Africa does not stand alone. Divinity and humanity, sacred and profane, visible and invisible are not perceived in isolation but in relation.

These elements are always interacting. Dualism in some cases has little or no place in African thought pattern. When the title of this book talks about African spiritual experience, this has to be contextualized. The experience being analysed is specific to Sub-Saharan African countries which to some extent share some similarities in cultural and religious expressions.

African Religion is something embedded in every sphere of African life. Religion permeates every aspect of African life. For some western academicians, they term this approach as African superstition. African religion and beliefs can be found in politics, economics and social and relational lives. Therefore, this book with its title does not touch on every aspect or the whole of African reality and religious lifestyle.

The title of this book gave me more room in my research when going through different materials and discourses that came my way. I am aware that there are other renowned academic scholars in Religious Anthropology in Africa, Sociology of Religion, Psychology of Religion, Social and Cultural Anthropology and African Religions and Philosophy who have profoundly researched and written on this subject. Therefore, the book draws its academic foundation on reference to the existing researched data and documentation. Furthermore, the book takes into consideration what is reported in the media. However, my contribution is an interpretation of the present religious environment as we are experiencing it today. This work is dependent on different references and works of different authors on different topics on African traditional religions to justify my interpretation of the current religious and spiritual experiences.

In narrowing the location of this book, it reflects more on the Zambian context in regard to religious experiences today. Zambia has been taken by the storm of religion. Zambia today is a place of different Christian expressions since 1991. The liberalization of the economy sent its tentacles in the "liberalization of Christianity".

Ever since, Zambia has had profound and extraordinary spiritual experiences. Zambia has experienced different religious leaders within and outside (DR Congo, South Africa, Zimbabwe, Nigeria, Ghana, Malawi, United States of America, Tanzania, Kenya and many other countries) with different approaches towards the spiritual and material challenges of many Zambians. Religious interaction of many Zambians with different realms, political, economic, medical, socio-cultural, of human life have become a point of interest to some scholars and academicians.

Division of the Book

The book is divided into six parts. The first part looks at the anthropological context of African life or world view. This part takes into account the source of logic of practice of African belief systems. This same part defines religion in general and in the context of colonization. African traditional religions are looked at by many people as a very peculiar reality in its expression and belief. However, there is no religion which is not peculiar. Every religion has its share of peculiarity in its beliefs and expressions.

In the second part, I have looked at the mythical landscape of Zambia's traditional belief system in relation to magic and witchcraft. In this part it has been argued that magic and witchcraft are some expressions and realities within the context of African belief system. These are part of belief system for an African whether we look at them from a negative point of view or irrational perspective.

The third part is about the reality of evil as understood in African traditional religions and life. This part looks at three main sources of evil in African belief systems. That is, God, the living dead or the ancestors and the living. The argument being made in this part is that evil emanates from poor and bad relationships with God, the living dead and the living.

The fourth part shades light on the centrality of rituals in African life. Nearly every important event in African life is punctuated with some religious ritual performance. This is so to connect the events, natural and human with the divine or the spiritual world. At the same time the sense of spiritual connectivity permeates every aspect of African life. There is no aspect that stands alone.

Every aspect is connected to the other at a deeper and spiritual level. Therefore, religious rituals are very central in African life for they connect events and experiences to the divine. It is this centrality that gives extraordinary authority to religious ritual leaders and specialists in African communities. Religious ritual specialists are like weavers working in the weaving room of African life. These weavers are an important aspect to African life.

Different life experiences are brought together. Religious rituals in this case connect the known to the unknown, the cooked to the uncooked, the inside to the outside, the cold to the hot, the lower to the higher, the near to the distant, the bush to the village, among others.

The fifth part interprets the fragmentation of African traditional religions in understanding the fragmentation of Christianity in Africa leading to different spiritual experiences today. These fragmentations and proliferations of different Christian churches are based on the importance of ritual and nature of African traditional religions which usually do not have permanent members.

It is this same centrality of rituals and nature of African traditional religions that give way to what western Christianity terms as "syncretism" though many Africans do not perceive it that way from an emic point of view.

The sixth and last part looks at how African traditional religions have domesticated the traditional Christian symbols to their own advantage. Christian symbols are not only seen from the perspective and meaning of Christianity as packaged by the western philosophy and logic but from African traditional religious point of view.

Chapter 1

Anthropological Context of African Life

Strictly by geographical and physical location all the peoples who trace their origin and live on the continent of Africa can be considered as Africans. That is persons who are of African ancestry, descendants and natives to Africa can be taken for granted as Africans. Today some have even gone further to define Africans as all those who are citizens of African Union. Membership to the African Union in this case has become a source of African identity and definition of Africa. This will include the White South Africans and the Arabs of the Mediterranean countries in the far North of Africa.

The term "African" however, has in practice come only to include primarily the indigenous peoples of Africa South of the Sahara, popularly known as the "Black Africans" which has more than 40 countries. It has to be pointed out that the terms, "Black- Africa" is contentious in its meaning, interpretation and application. To some it is a derogative way of describing Africa. When talking about Europeans, we do not refer them to as "White Europeans. They are just called Europeans. Why "Black Africans"? Sub-Saharan Africa is divided into Western Africa, Eastern Africa and Southern Africa. Each country in these areas has its own history, cultural, political scape or view with variety of ethnic groupings and languages.

It has to be mentioned that the term "black Africa" has its political and cultural argumentations which are not the basis of this discourse or discussion in this book. The basis for this assumption is not racially in nature but historical, cultural and geographical in outlook.[6]

Culturally, politically and historically many Africans North of the Sahara bear some differences with those of the South. Not only that, it has to be noted that many African countries, from a cultural point of view, have different cultural differentiations in terms of ethnic groupings, languages and tribes within their boundaries. Africa is a

---

[6] Thomas Sowell, Conquests and Cultures: An International History (New York: Basic Books, 1998), 99.

continent that prides in its rich cultural and religious differences of its peoples – plurality or diversity of cultures.

Cultural diversity and plurality can be experienced in many ways such as socio-political organizations and identifying and expression of authority, cultural and languages, approaches to cultural medicalization and healings, legal systems and dispute settlements, economic practices, religious expressions and beliefs, cultural spatial divisions, and many other important aspects.

Therefore, nothing can be taken for granted in Africa when it comes to cultural diversity, religious pluralism and general orientation. Africa is a witness to different cultures across its continent. At the same time Africa has different expressions of its religious experiences and beliefs. These expressions mainly include Christianity, Islam and African traditional religions. At the same time, it has to be mentioned that Africa has some traces of Hinduism and Jewish religions as well.

Christianity and Islamic religions today in Africa have in excess of 250 million followers each.[7] Within these there are further differences that can be experienced in terms of various expressions of Christianity and Islamic beliefs. Among Christians today we have the traditional Christian churches, prophetic, fundamentalists, Protestantism, Charismatic, among others. In Islam, we have the prominent expressions of Sufism and Salafism. Sufism has many followers and orders in West Africa and the Sudan. Salafism is relatively recent but has started spreading speedily in Africa.

African cultural diversity gives rise to diverse traditional religions and beliefs. This is true with Christianity and Islam too. Expression and success of Christianity and Islam go with particular cultures of people in given environments but with great respect to the fundamentals of respective religions.

Africa is rich in geographical differences and cultural diversity which applies as well to its traditional religions. Africa has a variety of traditional religions because of differences in cultures of its peoples. Even when we are talking about "African cosmology" we are not talking about one or single and defined cosmology.

---

[7] *Encyclopedia*, "Politics and African Religious Traditions", https://www.encyclopedia.com/environment/encyclopedia-almancs-transcripts-and-maps/politics-and-religion-politics-and-african-relious-traditions. Accessed on 2.09.2019.

When we are talking about "African cosmology" we are referring to a cosmological framework or a theoretical framework that brings together many different concepts and fundamental similarities which can be found in African traditional cultures and religions.

African cosmology in our discourse is a reference to a common "African-ness" in terms of cultures, traditions and religions. African cosmology like any other cosmology of people is an imprint on the minds of African people which is irrevocable belief in spiritual realities. It becomes very difficult to eradicate no matter how opposed to western logic or reason it may be. Cosmological beliefs and influences are hard to eradicate or to change in spite that they are socially hereditary in nature.

They become part of the human embodiment and habitus. They are influences or beliefs that are passed-on from one generation to another through deposits of knowledge in form of songs, sayings, proverbs, traditional fables and stories, storytelling, annual celebrations, ritual practices, belief systems, names of things and people, poems, sharing beliefs, conversations, thought patterns and inspirations through personal experiences.

It is no longer arguable that Africa and Zambia in particular have different traditional ethnic groupings with unique and particular ways of approaching, interpreting and looking at the world. Looking at the world and making interpretations of life events differ from one cultural group to another.

I remember some years ago, being in a foreign country in Europe, when we were invited at some social function as an African community comprising of Tanzanians, Zambians, Ugandans and Kenyans and we were requested to perform some traditional dance from Africa.

We could not do it not because we felt as objects of European guess but because we could not find a common dance and language to use among ourselves. Some people present could not believe it that we could not do a common dance since we were all Africans coming from the same continent of Africa.

For many Europeans, African culture is the same everywhere including dances, aesthetics, language and traditional practices. Their approach indicated that from their point of view, there are no cultural differentiations among Africans since Africa is one continent.

Few people with a better understanding of plurality of cultures would take it for granted that a group of Europeans coming from the continent of Europe will have the same culture and traditional practices. The French have some unique and particular cultural practices that are unique to them if compared to the British, Irish or the Germans or the Italians, Spanish, Portuguese.

At a certain level they share certain popular practices but that does not make them to be the same on fundamental cultural orientations. It is generally and politically-correct to talk about a "European Culture" or "Western Culture" but this should not overlook some cultural specifics across different European or Western cultural diversities.

People from the Eastern Europe for example, have unique cultures and practices compared to those in the Western Europe or Southern Europe. On many occasions Europeans have failed to apply the same understanding to the continent of Africa.

This differentiation among the Europeans can even be attested in their approach in the colonization of their particular regions and colonies before the African countries became independent and elsewhere across the global and continents, Asia, Americans, among others. Their economic, political and social colonization approaches were very different in styles, logic of practice and approaches.[8] Even their languages were different including language metaphors and symbolic expressions of communications. This is evident from different influences in terms of political, cultural, economic and infrastructures they have left behind in their former colonies.

The French approach was very different from the British including the aspects and instruments of dehumanizing of the local people. Some colonialists were more dehumanizing towards the colonized than others. In some colonies more local people died at the hands of the colonizers than others because of differences in brutal approaches.

This is true about the Belgian Congo, today called the Democratic Republic of the Congo (DRC). Others were more accommodating of the colonized and sharing their culture than others who were more in the "us" and "them" approach. Even in terms of the embedded cultures in infrastructures and division of space, differed from one colony to another. Others have left good infrastructure than others.

---

[8] John Gledhill, Power and its Disguises: Anthropological Perspectives on Politics (London: Pluto Press, 1994), 74.

Sometimes the organization of colonies depended on the local cultures, resistance and local political organizations of the local people. Some used some ethnic groups against others which have left certain African countries polarized politically leading to ethnic violence and socio-economic and political disparities being experienced today.

However, this does not absorb past and present African leadership from their responsibilities and contributions to the present political and economic challenges Africa is going through due to poor, mediocre leadership, maladministration of resources, political manipulation and corruption.

This happened even in the earliest religious missionary evangelizations. Some missionaries preferred to recruit more of the local church leaders from specific ethnic groups than from others. There are certain traditional Christian churches that thrived among specific ethnic groups for different reasons ranging from cultural, loyalty and submissiveness of the local political organizations.

Of course, this can be argued on the basis of different reasons ranging from the point of view of the local people and their cultures to colonial approaches towards the local people. The tensions and the imbalances are being felt today as a reaction to these historical imbalances. In certain traditional Christian churches in Africa today, you still find dominance of one or two ethnic groupings in general church membership and leadership. This is true also in some African countries regarding the holding of political and economic capital and dominance by certain ethnic groupings. Certain spheres are dominated by specific ethnic groups in some cases like politics, civil service, the army and the police.

In the more segmented and cultural pluralized societies like Zambia colonialism took the indirect political approach through the already established local political social structures and establishments, like the local chiefs and leadership. In the case of Zambia, the governance system was through what was called the Native Authorities, founded on indigenous institutions and socio-political structures.

The Native Authorities had the duty of maintaining law and order, collecting taxes and good governance among the natives through the local structures on behalf of the colonialists.⁹ This was the easiest way of governing vast territories with millions of people of different linguistic and cultural background at the same time keeping expenditure and staffing to a minimum.

In some acephalous societies like that of the Lenje, Ila and Tonga with different political and religious systems, there was imposition of traditional leadership by the colonialists in order to make the native authorities uniform throughout the territory.

This involved the arbitrary grouping of self-governing villages into new chiefdoms and imposed "traditional" ruling clans to serve the interests of the colonialists. These native authorities became tools for efficiency of colonial administration. There was proper subjugation of local leadership through colonial conquest and political domination.¹⁰ This killed political plurality of the local people. This was the beginning of centralized authorities leading to the formation of national states and central governments. This approach destroyed the plurality of governance among different local groupings in their local spaces.

In some colonies, for example of the French, they used the direct political approach of governance systems because of the existence of different cultural and political structures of local leadership.

This centralized and principle of direct administration for increased production and easy administration of colonies. This indicates the plurality of cultures of the African people, an element not respected by the colonialists. What is being mentioned at the continental level is as well true at each country level too. Zambia "officially" has seventy-two ethnic groups and different languages. It cannot be taken for granted that bringing together randomly five

---

⁹ Report on the effects of migratory labour in Northern Rhodesia, no title and year. Going through the whole report, this should have been a document submitted to the colonial authorities about the new way of life of a Native with the coming in of industrial life in the mines on the Copperbelt. This attests to the fact that colonialism and Christianity were intertwined. And both disregarded the culture of the people. Both were aimed at uprooting an African from his culture and traditions to become like a white man. This is an illusion to change people in such a way.

¹⁰ Gatian F. Lungu, ed. "Administrative Decentralization in Zambian Bureaucracy: An Analysis of Environmental Constraints", Lusaka: University of Zambia Institute for African Studies, *Zambian Papers* No. 18, (1985), 29; Lewis H. Gann, The Birth of a Plural Society: The Developments of Northern Rhodesia under the British South Africa Company (Manchester: Manchester University Press, 1958), 98 – 99.

people from different ethnic groups they will be able to perform a common traditional dance since they are all Zambians. Zambia is country of cultural differentiations in out-look and practice.

Even the success of European evangelization was very much dependent on different cultural organization of the local people and their traditional religions. Some Christian Euro-evangelizations quickly succeeded in some parts of the African local communities and societies than others. The Catholic Church for example, in the 19th century initially failed in some parts of Southern and Western parts of Zambia.

The same Catholic Church succeeded in the Luapula, Northern and Copperbelt provinces. This was due partly to the different approaches of the Christian Euro-evangelization churches and the different cultural and religious organizations of the local people.

For Copperbelt Province the reasons for the success of early evangelization may be different. Most of the people on the Copperbelt had migrated from Luapula and Northern provinces of Zambia where they had already been introduced to Catholic Christian faith by the early missionaries in those parts of Zambia. Christianity for migrants on the Copperbelt served as a new kinship in the fragmented cultural life of capitalism and individualism.

This can be true even today to some extent. Christianity serves as an instrument of social cohesion in the socially and politically fragmented capitalistic societies where people have lost a sense of identity and threatened by individualism. In some cases, it's the entrenchment of the local people in their cultural traditions, practices and beliefs which made the early Christian evangelization to experience challenges in taking root. In some regions like South Africa, lack of rootedness of Christianity was due to the growing religious, economic and political alienation and marginalization enhanced by racism and land expropriation which led the local people to find religious meaning in Zionism, an independent African Christian church.[11]

This is true as well about the success of Christianity in the Eastern part of Africa among the Dinka, Maasai, Luo and the Kikuyu peoples. The successes of Christianity among and in each of these different

---

[11] Gledhill, Power and its disguises: Anthropological Perspective on Politics, 83 – 85.

groups of people are different due to differences in cultures of these people and their local structural organizations.

Among the Maasai for example, Christianity found it difficult to find roots partly because of the cultural way of life and the belief system of the people. This is also true with the Khoisan people of southern Africa where their cultural and society organization made it difficult for Christianity to find roots in this cultural milieu of the Khoisan people.

Christianity has failed to be firmly rooted in many African societies because of the nature of the cultural life and belief systems of the local people. Some cultural, social structures and belief systems were more receptive to Christianity compared to others.

Others took a lukewarm stand of accommodating Christianity because they were suspicious of the agents of Christianity while others never saw anything new in the new religion. Other traditional religions could not perceive anything new in the new religion and therefore, the new religion meant nothing and had nothing new to offer to the local people.

All these interpretations offer a window of understanding African cosmology or world-view on approaches to African life as experienced today. Like any other people in the world, Africans are deeply rooted in their African cosmology and perspectives of the world around them. Perception and interpretation of the world that surround them is influenced from this point of view.

1.1. Differentiations among African Cultures

Talking about African culture and its world-view or cosmology from such an angle of seeing African culture as being the same everywhere in Africa could be a fallacy because that is not what the reality of Africa is.[12] The reality is that Africa is composed of many different, unique cultures and ethnicities. This per- se makes it difficult to talk about "African culture" as specific, common and the same for the whole of Africa.

There is nothing like "African culture" in reality which is applicable to all Africans. There are different opinions as to whether one should speak of "African culture" or "African cultures" in terms

---

[12] Susan Vogel, Baule: African Art in Western Eyes (New Haven: Yale University Press, 1997), 228-229.

of African values or ethnic values. Egbulem argues that we can still find sufficient reasons for holding to what can be termed as "common Africanness" or some basic world-view among Africans which according to him is true for the entire sub-Saharan Africa.[13] This region of Africa shares some fundamental commonness that can be referred to as African culture.

There is no one and common defined culture in Africa which we can call with certainty as "African culture". There could be some similarities on some elements of culture among certain African ethnic groupings but this does not mean and lead to the conclusion that there is a common African culture.[14] Different African ethnic cultural groupings may have some similar practices, beliefs, values and traditions but not what we can call a common shared culture in totality.

Could it be that the concept of "African culture" finds its origin in the western conceptualization in the definition of Africa? Is it another way of describing "African culture" by a Westerner without any regard to specifics and variations of cultures in Africa due to ignorance? There has always been this approach towards Africa which looks at Africa as a single entity in terms of culture and traditional practices.

One should not take it for granted that bringing a Zambian, Tanzanian, Ugandan and Kenyan together would be able to perform a common African cultural dance since they are coming from the same continent – Africa. This is being ignorant of African cultural reality and its cultural diversity. Of course, there is in every society, what we can call "popular cultures" which are shared by many in terms of ideas, knowledge, information, creative works, principles, entertainments, music, sports and style. The argument being posited here is that the issue of "African culture" can be heavily contested in academic world. For some their arguments for "African-ness" extends even to the Africans across the Atlantic- "African – Americans" who share some origins and some religious similarities

---

[13] Chris, Nwaka, Egbulem, "African Spirituality", *The New Dictionary of Catholic Spirituality*, ed. Michael Downey (Bangalore: Theological Publications in India, 1995), 20.

[14] Peter K. Sapong, People Differ (Accra: Sub-Saharan Publishers, 2002), 38-39; Benjamin C. Ray, African Religions: Symbol, Ritual and Community (New Jersey: Prentice hall, 2000), ix.

with some Africans still living on the main land continent of Africa. And arguments on this discourse abounds.[15]

It is not wrong to consider "African – Americans" as Africans. That is a reality and a fact." African – Americans" are Africans at the same time it is not wrong to consider them Americans, that is what they are too. While for some, only specifically consider "African culture" those African cultures found only on the continent of Africa.

Others exclude the cultures of Africans living between the Sahara Desert and the Mediterranean Sea from African culture – known as Mediterranean culture. Mediterranean culture can be argued as partly African culture because it is found on the continent of Africa.

This diversity of cultures is not only a case of Africa in general as a continent but even of individual African countries. Some African countries have different ethnic groupings speaking different languages and very unique in many ways, such that you may not combine them and come up with one culture, for example, a "Zambian culture" for all Zambians.

Though there is an academic claim and proof that, some societies from the equator down to the Cape of Good Hope, at the tip of southern Africa, under which Zambia falls geographically, are grouped by linguists as speakers of interrelated Bantu languages, that trace their origins from west Africa, the area between Cameroun and Nigeria, this should not be culturally construed or taken for granted to mean they are the same people in reference to cultural orientation.

It has to be hastened to mention that till now there is no archaeological and genetic conclusive evidence to support this trace. However, there is some evidence that these regions show some extensive similarities in language and cultural symbolic similarities.

However, this should not be over simplified or exaggerated to mean the same culture. They have some common and basic assumptions and institutionalized behaviours in the fields of etiology, religious expressions, philosophy, language, traditional medical diagnosis, interpretations and therapy. Theses do not imply that they have a common culture but share certain cultural traits and commonalities. These differentiations in cultures applies as well to traditional religions.

---

[15] Lewis R. Gordon, Existential Africana (New York: Routledge, 2000), 144 – 145.

Africa is a home to different cultural groupings and belief systems. This makes it impossible to talk about "African traditional religion" as if it exists as a single coherent body of beliefs and practices. When we are talking about religion in African context we talk in terms of "African traditional religions", in the plural.

African traditional religions exist in their various forms because of the rich African cultural diversity. There is no existence of creed or doctrine to summarize the African belief systems in respect to African religion. It is a religion that is based on oral transmission, rituals, and practices and imbedded in life as it is lived every day. It is not a "religion of the book" like Christianity, Jewish and Islam with their respective books of reference, the Bible, the Tora and the Quran.

African traditional religion is a religion that is written on people's hearts and life. It is written in the minds, oral history, rituals, names, philosophical concepts, metaphors and symbols, shrines and religious functions and ceremonies - life.

It has no founders or reformers the way it is with Gautama, the Buddha, Christ or Mohammed. It has no orientation of missionaries, propagation or proselytizing.[16] Of course Africa has had some traditional religious prophets galvanizing people through religion for some causes and challenging situations and realities.

Good examples are the South African figures in the personalities of Soga and Dukwana, among the Xhosa people, Simon Kimbangu the founder of the Kimbanguist religious movements in the DR Congo (Zaire) and Harris the founder of Harrist Church in Ivory Coast.[17] Even then these prophets never came up with definable and coherent belief systems and doctrines to be followed and win more adherents to their new found faith.

A cause is identified to be addressed by the community, in this case renewing the Christian faith based on African values and

---

[16] Joseph Osmosade Awolalu, "What is African Traditional Religion," www.studies comparative religion.com/public/article/what is_african_traditional-religion-by-josephosmosade-awolalu.aspx. Accessed on 10.06.2019.

[17] Janet, Hodgson, "The Africanization of missionary Christianity: history and typology", *Journal of Religion in Africa*, Vol. XVI – 3 (1986): pg. 187 – 208; D.J. Mackey, "Simon Kimbangu and the B.M.S. tradition", *Journal of Religion in Africa*, Vol. XVII – 2 (1987), 113 – 171; David A. Shank, "The Harrist church in the Ivory Coast" (Review Article), *Journal of Religions in Africa*, Vol. XV – 1 (1985), 67 – 75.

traditions. These are some of the peculiarities and uniqueness of African traditional religions.

This desire and need to be accepted and understood about Africa Christian religion, just as Pope Francis(Catholic religion) and the grand Imam of Al-Azhar, Ahamad Al-Tayyeb (Islamic religion) have acknowledged the existence of different religions in the world through an important document for the creation of world peace:

> "The pluralism and diversity of religions, color, sex, race and language are willed by God in his wisdom, through which he created human beings".[18]

The same document quoted above recognizes and accepts the plurality and diversity of religions among different peoples of the world, which in many cases have been denied by world religions for a long time. The same document rejects the forcing of other people of different religions to adhere to certain religions or cultures.

Meaning that a particular culture should not be imposed on other cultures which are different. Here respect for "pluralism and diversity" of cultures and religions are a key for peace in the world.[19] This is not the belief held by Christianity and Islam for a long time. Christianity and Islam believe to be the only true religions and the whole world has to be converted to Christianity by the Christians and to Islam by the Muslims.

That is why this document has been condemned by some sections of Catholic leadership because it is thought to put Christianity on the same level with other religions instead of being at the higher level. This document implies that religions like African traditional religions are also willed by God and therefore, they deserve respect and existence in their totality.

For a long time, Christianity has condemned African traditional religions as being pagan and for uncivilized. This has played on the

---

[18] w2.vatican.va/content/francesco/en/travels/2019/outside/documents/papa-francesco_20190204_documento-fratellanza-umana.html. Accessed on 27.08.2019.

[19] w2.vatican.va/content/francesco/en/travels/2019/outside/documents/papa-francesco_20190204_documento-fratellanza-umana.html. Accessed on 27.08.2019.

minds of Africans to be repugnant to their own positive African beliefs and ultimately to their own African cultures and identities.

At the same time, when we are talking about African cultures, it has to be realized, recognized and accepted that the cultures found in Africa have had influences and admixtures from other people's cultures from both within,(endogenous) and outside-(exogenous) cultures, Africa for a very long time.[20] The meeting of different indigenous African cultures with the exogenous cultures is not an innocent one.

There is an interpenetration of cultures that give rise to changes and enrichment, losing and gaining. This is true as well with African traditional religions, Christianity and Islam. African traditional religions have been influenced by Christianity and Islam and vice versa in a great deal by African traditional religions in their expression and practice.

Therefore, what may be termed as "African culture" may not be purely African but a mixture of different cultural accommodations from other outside cultures of other people. There is no culture in this case that can claim innocence, purity and originality.

Not even the Christian culture can claim that it is purely Christian culture. In any case what is a "pure Christian culture"? Christianity over the centuries has accommodated elements from the ancient Middle-East and European cultures, some of which were considered as "pagan" through diffusion, cultural inter-course and sharing of the common environment.

Diffusion is the passing on of cultural traits found in one culture and society into another. And many cultural practices claimed by specific cultural groupings have actually originated from other cultures and societies through the process of cultural interaction and inter-course. Therefore, there is no human culture that can claim to be pure and original in its state of existence.

Environment (physical, socio-economic, cultural, political) is another aspect believed to dictate and affect the way of life of people. Sometimes people who share some common physical environments are likely to share some similarities in social life.[21] Physical

---

[20] Didier N. Kaphagawani and Jeanette G. Malherebe, "African Epistemology", *The African Philosophy Reader*, ed. Pieter H. Coetzee and Abraham P.J. Roux (New York: Routledge, 1998), 212.

[21] Marvin, Harris, Culture, People, Nature: An Introduction to General Anthropology, 7th ed. (New York: Longman, 1997), 93 – 94.

environment can influence Socio-cultural and religious life of the people.

This is true about Zambia and how the capitalistic environment has impacted on the culture and religious life of the people – Christianity based on prosperity and giving answers to lack of prosperity. This is so because Christianity is operating in an environment were to prosper is part of modern life. Wealth and prosperity notions have been engraved in religious belief system. Christianity has taken into account the ideas of wealth and prosperity in religious experiences to give meaning to daily life of people.

However, there is nothing wrong in speaking about "African culture" if one is giving a discourse about a particular culture which is specific to Africa's unique ethnic group of people.

Every African culture in this case that is specific to an ethnic group of people living in Africa is therefore, an "African culture". It therefore, follows that what is "African culture" should not be taken for granted.

For example, there are intricacies of differentiations among Africans in understanding of a family and authority, relationships and relations, kinship and approaches to gender, interpretations of space, beliefs and values, socio-cultural and political organizations, public and private, beginning of human life and fertility, relationships with the divine or transcendent, social responsibilities, law and settlement of conflicts or disputes, socialization and education.[22] These indicate variations in what we term, "African culture".

That is why thinking that the challenges of Africa be it political, economic or social can be addressed from a monolithic western premise is unattainable. This was the failure of Economic Structural Adjustment Programme (ESAP) tailored by the International Monetary Fund (IMF) for African countries in the 1970s - 1990s.

The same programme was applied in the same way to different countries with different cultural, economic, political and social structural backgrounds. Sometimes, unfortunately, African challenges, economic, political, socio-cultural have been approached from this monolithic and linear stance.

---

[22] Klaus E. Muller and Ute Ritz-Muller, Soul of Africa – Magical Rites and Traditions (Maxeville: Konemann, 2000), 10-17.

It has to be accepted that there is no single formula that can be applied to all African countries in solving African challenges.[23] In short, there is no single straight jacket to fit all African countries in addressing their challenges and problems. Not even a uniform religious belief system can address African religious challenges. Application of monolithic and linear models is only good for re-colonization and controlling people.

This is true even when it comes to Christianity. Applying the same model of Christianity to different African ethnic groups and societies may not give the same out-come. This is like the application of the same model (economic, political or social) to all African countries by international bodies. Such models are effective for re-colonization of Africa and not for human progress and development.

Africa is one of the victims of application of the same foreign models to its uniqueness of various cultures. This application of the same models to different African societies may explain the failure of the same models.

Can this explain why there is a proliferation of churches in Africa, as a reaction to the application of the same models of Christianity to plural cultures? Proliferation of Christian churches becomes a yearning for different ways of expressing Christianity based on cultural contexts of people. Proliferation of Christian churches is a search for religious identity and meaningful belief system.

The same linear approach was applied even in the evangelization process by some traditional Christian missionary churches. Religiously the "heathens" (Africans in this case) were considered in this process to be people gone astray and caught up in extreme vices, people without a culture, without history and caught up in "primitivism".

Culturally and religiously Africans were considered backward in need of a forward push. Missionaries and colonialists who came into Africa portrayed Africans as pagans and savages. Civilization and Christianization in this case went hand in hand and became so intertwined and closely knit. The work of civilization was seen not only as the work of colonial administration, but also as an instrument in the hands of missionaries.

---

[23] Lionel, Cliffe, "African Renaissance," *Africa in Crisis: New Challenges and Possibilities*, ed. Tunde Zack-Williams, Diane Frost and Alex Thomson (London: Pluto Press, 2002), 41.

Names from African tradition were disparaged in Christian religion. The herbalist was condemned as a "witchdoctor", rituals were forbidden including drums. Herbalist, the witch, witch-finder, diviner, witchdoctor and a traditional priest were considered to be the same – evil and pagan. Africans were taught to turn their back on their cultures and belief systems and become cultured through Christianity and embracing of the culture and religion of the colonial master.

Colonial evangelism can be seen from two perspectives in this case. Firstly, colonial evangelism as an encounter between local and global aimed at converting "savages" into pious peasants and citizens of Christendom. It was aimed at "de-culturizing" an African by removing them from their roots and their African authenticity and making them citizens of Christianity and God's children.

The expectations of the missionaries were for an African to turn his back to his culture, way of life and belief system. It was a project of whitening the "black mind" and framing his mind in western culture, logic, philosophy and theology.

Secondly, colonial evangelism can be perceived as an agent of seeding a pervasive new order that would together with other colonizing forces make Africans into impoverished, loyal, subordinated subjects of the empires, dependent on their masters and making them tools of economic development. These two levels reinforced one another.

Christianity saw itself as having a task of registering new structural embodiments on the African body. Body work was an effort to tune the physical registers of dark persons through grooming, dress and comportment. This became a crucial mode of colonial product. This was as well one of the basic methods implicit in the mission by which the Christian missionary hoped to create a new moral order and empire.

A good example is how Christianity characterized the historical specific upheavals in Central South Africa caused by the rise of the Zulu state. These upheavals were perceived as "anarchy and misery" of people living in spiritual darkness. African way of life was considered as a moral chaos and without a moral campus:

> They had no marriage, nor any proper domestic order, nor acknowledged any moral obligation to the duties arising out of that relationship. Females were exchanged for others, bartered for cattle,

given as presents, and often discarded by the mere caprice of the men ... The absence of the proper domestic affections, and unnatural treatment of children ... has been in part started ... yet the divine institution has been introduced.[24]

Nothing of rationality, culture, moral and resembling common sense ever existed among Africans in terms of moral obligations, family life, kinship, raising of children, relationship between males and females and general cultural life among the Africans according to the western rationality and perception.

Everything was seen as irrational and without even a speck of common sense. This perception was due to the fact that Christianity never understood the logic of practice of African people in their social contexts and cultural environment. The approach of Christianity was to obliterate this irrational culture and replace it completely with Christian normative and its moral order. This was and is still a failed project of Christianity – replacing African belief system completely with Christian culture.

Colonization and Evangelism became instruments for creating a new African, with a culture, history and at the same time ideal tools with which to educate and discipline the African in becoming a good citizen and be firmly rooted in European and Christian cultures.

For example, a report on the challenges of migratory labour and its effects in Northern Rhodesia coming from Monsignor Mazzierri talks about the benefits of industrial life on evangelization (appendix 1). This indicates the linkage between colonial civilization and the project of evangelization. Among the benefits listed are the following;

a. **Discipline:** - A native was considered undisciplined and idle human being who was supposed to be submitted and exposed to a life of order and work through industrialization. That through this an African was taught to rise at a fixed hour and be at work. The strenuous work in the mines made the native shake off the natural apathy and laziness and became physically strong.

---

[24] Broadbent Samuel, A Narrative of the First Introduction of Christianity amongst the Barolong Tribe of Bechuanas, South Africa: With a brief Summary of the subsequent History of the Wesleyan Mission to the same People (London: Wesleyan Mission House: 1865), 203 – 204.

Even the church saw an African as a disordered and lazy person. Evangelization was seen partly as a project of ordering the life of an African. Evangelization was supposed to partly discipline the body, mind and soul of an African – regimentalizing an African through discipline. This worked well for colonization of an African. Evangelization became a tool and urgent of colonization. There was a certain interdependent between colonization and evangelization. Colonial administration of the local people depended on the Christian evangelization and evangelization on the colonial administration for disciplining an African.

b. **Hygiene and Cleanliness:** - An African was seen as a being that lacked bodily hygiene and cleanliness including the surrounding. Through industrialization the dirty and badly dressed Native soon realized the benefit of washing, bathing and sanitary accommodation. An African was moved from natural into a culture state. Even among the earliest explorers, hygiene and discipline were interlinked in the approach to colonization. Hygiene was considered as a matter of discipline. Hygiene was an explicit way in which the colonial powers exercised their regimentation of African people. Thus, hygiene became part of the sentimental and emotional inner life. It included among other things, clothing, sanitary housing and healthy food.[25] Before that there was no culture in Africa but only nature. These were the benefits for evangelization that came from industrialization of Northern Rhodesia. Value of education was seen in terms of civilizing, instilling new skills, notions of individual responsibility, morality, value of work, time, order and cleanliness.[26]

c. **Religiously:** - An African was considered as having no religious sense, if anything it was based on suspicions and ancestral worship as an end in itself. Industrialization improved the religious life of a Native because the Native now lived closer to the mission which was the centre of civilization. Through Christian teaching and assistance from the missionaries, an African and the aversion to

---

[25] Johannes Fabian, Out of our Minds: Reason and Madness in the Exploration of Central Africa (London: University of California Press, 2000), 78.

[26] Karen Tranberg Hansen, "Cookstove and Charcoal Braziers", *African Encounters with Domesticity*, ed. Karen Tranberg Hansen (New Jersey: Rutgers University Press, 1992), 269.

others was brought into check. Through Christian teaching, an African developed a better feeling in mind towards others which never existed before. The brutal nature of an African according to this was brought into check. The savage mind of an African was domesticated by introducing a new religion of peace based on the scripture and Holy book. Even Christianity saw an African as a savage and a beast that needed redemption.

This clearly indicates that even Christianity was part of the grand project of changing the culture of an African.[27] Colonial administration used religion indirectly and subtly as an instrument of pursuing social and political domination. European missionary churches in this way became an important facet of colonial cultural domination. Christianity in this way had an ambiguous contradictory symbolic power of repression and liberation, freedom and subjugation. It aimed at religious liberty for an African, liberation of the soul of an African for high religion at the same time wiping out primitive culture and replacing it with western culture.

It became a religion of contradictions. Christianity and colonization were considered the dawning of new history, civilization and a new world – order for an African.

Missionaries and colonialists in many ways encouraged Africans to change their, identity, behaviour and attitudes in hygiene, time-bound notions, and gender relations in respect of private home and labour, including dressing.[28] Uniforms were introduced for different groups of people, servants, clerks and messengers.

This was the same in Christianity up-to today. This was part of regimentalization of local people. The society was organized according to strict, passive, oppressive systems or patterns. The above approach of Christianity made it part of the web of the civilization mission for an African. At the same time, it must not be overlooked that but acknowledged that some Christian missionaries also paved way for the dislodging of colonialism in some way.

A mission station was considered to be a symbolic centre of civilization and villages later came to cluster around the mission

---

[27] Appendix 1, In the Report on the Effects of migratory labour in Northern Rhodesia.
[28] Karen Tranberg Hansen, "Introduction: Domesticity in Africa", in Karen Tranberg Hansen, 11.

stations and became very powerful symbols of modernity, new culture, new belief system and civilization.

Existence of the mission centres acted as centres of cultural and social power for conquering the African pagan culture. A mission station was not only a symbolic representation of "heaven" but western culture and its civilizing mission. It served as a contact space with new western culture.

A mission centre was an instrument of confrontation and containment of backward African culture. A mission station stood as an architectural symbol of civilization.

Even today to some extent the Euro-Christian traditional church centres are perceived and considered as symbols of power especially with their imposition of huge church structures and Cathedrals in the centres of towns. President Edgar Chagwa Lungu of Zambia, in attacking the "traditional Christian Churches", who turned down the attendance of National Dialogue Forum, said that is not in having big Cathedrals that some churches were holier (Powerful) than others. It was an indirect reference to Euro-traditional churches like the Catholic Church, United Church of Zambia and the Anglican Church.

This was when the president was asked to comment about the absence of the "traditional Christian Churches" at the National Dialogue Forum (NDF) which took place in 2019. In the mind of the president a Cathedral is still a symbol and representation of power.

The invitation in some way to comment on the absence of the "Church" was like reminding the president about the symbolic power of the "Church". This has been the general symbolic perception of people of some Euro-Christian traditional churches and some churches see themselves as such.

Religious institutions for a long time have been considered as spaces of symbolic power. These institutions have the symbolic power to control, influence and manipulate people. That is why the irrationality of certain manipulations and activities in these institutions have to be evaluated from this background of symbolic power.

Religious institutions will always remain for a long-time to come spaces of contested power from within and without. For a long-time people who have not submitted to western Christian beliefs have been considered uncivilized and evil. That is why such kind of people were even referred to as "pagans" – "abasenshi". This term carries with it derogative connotation, like being far from the grace of God, people of darkened minds who are damned.

Mission stations became symbolic centres of power for conquering uncivilized mind and life of an African. They were considered to be light in the midst of darkness. And a missionary was considered to be a mystical being from a very far away and different world of abundance.

This interpretation added some mysticism to missionary evangelization. These civilizing centres contrasted between the known (mission) and the unknown (African villages), the civilized (Western culture) and the uncivilized (local culture), culture and nature, enlightened and the primitive, believer and pagan, the tamed and the untamed, refined and the raw, light and darkness.

Later in the years the blank space of the African continent had to be mapped to give it modern western geographical identity. This was done through the Berlin conference which took place from November 15, 1884 to February 26, 1885 also known as the Berlin West- Africa Conference (BWAC) or the Congo Conference.

The wild African land had to be tamed and cultivated culturally, politically and religiously. The pitiable-suffering lot had to be saved.[29] The boundaries of the Berlin conference never respected the local differences, alliances, affiliations, family ties of the local people in terms of languages and culture.

As a result, the issue of boundaries has remained a nightmare up to today between and among some of the new states and among tribal boundaries. Some people found themselves cut off from their kingdoms and traditional cultural centres. Cultural centres were replaced by Christian church centres or stations and what were known as "Boma".

The Church centres and the "Boma" usurped the powers of the local authorities and cultures. The more far away people lived from the missions, the more uncivilized they were considered to be. A mission station became partly part of the social and cultural identity of the people.

Though there is a lot of appreciation of what industrialization and Christianity brought, the approach, depiction and description of an

---

[29] Jean Comaroff and John L. Comaroff "Home-Made Hegemony", in Karen Tranberg Hansen, 40.

African life leaves much to be desired. It is the painting of an African "wholly black", and without a culture and sense of religion and spirituality which was and has been negative. African traditional religions were denigrated as un-evolved compared to the Western religions and with no civilizations.

Some had not even visited Africa but spoke with authority on Africa in very derogative and negative way. A good example is, Leo Frobenius who had just heard narratives about Africa from travellers and adventurers and went ahead and wrote in the Berlin journal:

> Before the introduction of genuine faith and higher standards of culture by the Arabs, the Natives had neither political organization nor strictly speaking any religion ... Therefore, in examining the pre-Muhammadan conditions of the negro races, to confine ourselves to the description of their crude fetishism, their brutal and often cannibal customs, their vulgar and repulsive idols and their squalid homes ...[30]

Some even doubted whether an African could comprehend the concept of God as a philosophical concept.[31] An African was seen as a person without the concept of God.

In reality, contrary and in contrast to these negative notions, an African had a concept of the supreme-being. It is only the approach to the supreme-being that was different from the westerner. Like Idowu, this can be characterized as a "period of ignorance and false certainty" from the west.[32]

According to a Catholic priest, Schmidt of Vienna, who is mentioned by Evans Pritchard, who worked among the pygmies of the Congo in central Africa he believed that the truth is that there exists no known people who are totally devoid of culture and religion.[33] Therefore, Africans had a concept of God, spirituality and explained his existence and his being in a totally different way from the western philosophical conception and mind.

---

[30] Leo Frobenius, *The voice of Africa*, Vol.1, (Hutchison, 1913), xii. Actually, Frobenius had not even visited Africa before writing this about Africa.

[31] Edwin William Smith, ed., African Ideas of God (London: Edinburgh House Press, 1966), 1.

[32] Bolaji E. Idowu, African Traditional Religions A Definition (London: S.C.M. Press, 1973), 88.

[33] Evans Pritchard, Theories of Primitive Religion (Oxford: Oxford University Press, 1965), 103ff.

Out of ignorance of the westerners, Africans were people caricatured as involved in superstition, animism and ancestral worship.[34] Not only that, for a long time African continent was seen and considered as a continent without history. History begun with the advent and coming in of colonialism, for Africa was considered a dark continent and darkness is not a subject of historical discourse and analysis.[35]

The only history that existed and taught in Africa was the European history with a perspective that served the European agenda. Learning of European history and geography became obligatory in African education systems in restructuring the mind of an African and to introduce an African and insert him in the paradigm of Western identity.

This was to introduce an African to a new world, civilization and real history of the civilized people. It is only in recent years that African history has been emphasized in African education system, though with little encouragement and enthusiasm. Like colonial civilization, colonial evangelism has to be understood both as a cultural project in itself and as a metonym of a global civilizing movement. Its agents certainly saw themselves as an integral part of the grand imperial design.[36]

Christianity in Africa like Bourdieu puts it has for a long time been considered as a hegemony that has come to be taken for granted. It is partly a social construct that has come to permeate the African society. It has become partly a phenomenon that has been naturalized and cannot be contested openly.[37] However, it has to be understood that there is no hegemony that is total. Every hegemony is created and recreated, therefore contested.

It is only now that these mission centres have slowly started losing their social-cultural capital and symbolic power because sources of civilization and symbolic power have become multiple.

---

[34] Timothy, "African Traditional Religions", https://www.biblicaltraining.org/library/african-traditional-religion-in-practice/essentials-african-traditional-religions/timothy. Accessed on 11.06.2019.

[35] This was quoted by B.A. Ogot, Some Approaches to African History (Nairobi: Hadith 1, 1968), 1-2; Christopher Ehret, The Civilization of Africa: A history to 1800, n.d. (Oxford: James Currey, 2002), 3.

[36] John Comaroff and Jean Comaroff, Ethnography and Historical imagination (Oxford: Westview Press, 1992), 3-48.

[37] Pierre Bourdieu, Outline of a Theory of Practice (Cambridge and New York: Cambridge University Press, 1977), 94.

This is true with some of the earliest missionary centres. In spite of increase in population of people around them very few people identify themselves with these missionary centres anymore. In fact, the numbers of people who identify themselves with these centres of civilization have drastically dwindled. It was a civilization and a project without a future, a sense of permanence and identity.

Today sources of symbolic power of civilization include among others, the media, school, hospital, court, road, internet, shopping mall, civil association etc. Monopoly and relevance of the Euro-Christian traditional churches as civilizing symbolic powers are slowly diminishing.

Monopoly of symbolic power of Euro-Christian traditional churches is slowly slipping away. There is even contestation on powers of the "Boma".[38] Actually the "Boma" has become a failed project for manipulation, pillaging of resources, thieving and control of the people. In Africa the "boma" is characterized by brutality, violence and dictatorship for it to control the people. It is slowly taking on the model of the colonialist oppression to maintain order and resemblance of western civilization.

1.2. Colonization through Religion

There has always been this Marxist thinking of identifying Africa with nature and not with its history. This notion contrasts an African to the Western life and its philosophy. Africa is equated to nature while the West to culture. This is a pure denial of African history and culture by contrasting Africa to nature, while history and Europe are identified with culture and therefore, Europe has a history and a higher civilization.[39]

This is so because nature is often understood to remain relatively constant and uniform, while culture by its very nature changes. A human being has history because he is a cultural being. However, it is a fact that there is no known group of people in the world without a history, no matter how much they are close to nature.

---

[38] The New Oxford Dictionary of English, (1998), "Boma" is a Swahili name to describe an enclosure, especially for animals.

[39] Elspeth Huxley, The Sorcerer's Apprentice (London: Chatto and Windus, 1949), 89; Alberto Moravia, Which tribe do you belong to? (New York: Farrar, Straus and Giroux, 1976), 112.

Every group of people has its own civilization to be appreciated and respected. The thinking that civilization and progress are processes of development from nature to culture in relation to an African is somehow misplaced. Africans were seen as "less human", savages, violent, disorderly, without restraint, cheap labour or tools for the colonizers to use for enrichment. Therefore, European merchants and missionaries came as civilizing agents.

Foreign missionaries were encouraged to co-operate with the colonial governments to fulfil this civilizing project. The success of Christianity was tied to the firm rootedness and entrenchment of European colonialism in African local societies. The missionaries became partners with the western political and economic forces.

In this marriage between colonial administrators and missionaries, was considered as re-enforcement of a civilizing mission and project. Religious institutions were seen and considered as instruments of civilization.[40] However, it should not be easily forgotten that western world has been at the centre of savagery, violence, disorder, lack of restraint and descending into genocide and lynching of black people.[41]

It is unfortunate that there are still pockets of colonial approaches in Christianity where there is still no acceptance of African values and celebratory life as having a Spirit of Christ to be unveiled to make an African at home in living Christian life.

There is always this belief of bringing Christ into African culture which means that African culture is devoid of the spirit of Christ. It can be argued that the spirit of Christ is as well in African culture and yearning to be unveiled and to be made alive. There is no religion in the world that can bring and give the spirit of Christ to another. It can only awaken the spirit of Christ in another culture. There is no one culture that has the monopoly of the spirit of God.

The Catholic Church in Zambia is an example of a church which is deeply entrenched into its Western Roman Catholic Church culture with very little embracing of meaningful inculturation in the name of being part of the universal church. If anything, the church is even being pushed back to the purely ancient Roman Catholic Church as a renewal.

---

[40] Benezet, Bujo, African Theology: In its Social Context (Nairobi: Don Bosco Training Centre Printing Press, 2003), 38-42.

[41] Christopher Ehret, The Civilization of Africa: A history to 1800, n.d, 5.

That is doing things exactly as they are being done in Rome without paying attention to unique, fundamental and African cultural values. Christianity is still veiled in Christian colonial hung-over of Latinization, Romanization and Gregorianization of the Church. All these are prejudices against African culture and its civilizations.

Even drums, local language, local names, rituals, herbs and native songs were taken to be profane and pagan. African converts were expected to turn their backs on their cultures as a way of civilizing Africans. Of course, it has to be appreciated that most of the earliest missionaries who were sent to evangelize were not well schooled and prepared to experiencing differences in culture. They came with a romantic perception of Africa as a lost and Dark Continent in need of enlightenment.

It has to be understood today that civilization has to be understood in its plurality of cultures and differences. Every society has complex laws, rules unique social behaviours whether these rules and norms are written or oral. Societies are civilized in different ways. Today, it is proper to talk about Western, Islamic, African and Christian civilizations. Even within African civilization there are different civilizations like, Niger-Congo, Afrasan, Sudanic and Khoisan civilizations.[42] The term "civilization" in this case should not carry a tone of value judgment on the "other" when referring to the "other" – people who are different in many ways.

This was a colonial approach which led to the up-rooting of Africans from their socio-cultural, political and economic identity. In the past such mistakes were made in terms of Western Christian approaches, economic policies, political ideologies and education systems towards Africa.

For example, the orientation of the education systems in Africa till today are towards "whitening" of the individual person to reach a certain status, good job and very little about self – understanding, self-respect, self-appreciation, cultural identity, African values and tapping into the endogenous knowledge, creativity and skills.

The education systems in Africa for a long time have not equipped the young African scholars to tap into the moral, African values, economic, and political resource of the local or indigenous cultural logic. Education has continued to serve the purpose of the colonial

---

[42] Christopher Ehret, The Civilization of Africa: A history to 1800, 5-7.

endeavour, which is the colonization of the mind and disruption of African identity.

In the end the education systems in Africa have become a framework for social frustration, disappointment and illusion. It does not provide the "whitening" it promises in its clients. Education systems as we have them in most African countries are still straight-jackets and models prescribed for Africa based on western logic and philosophy.

The present African education systems do not take into consideration the local African cultures and the philosophies in which an African is embedded. In a case of Zambia frequent changes to education curriculum have destabilized the education system. It is all in search of education system that responds to the needs of the local people. These changes are compounded by what Luckson Saka calls, "grip of a quality crisis". The crisis includes poor educational infrastructure in rural areas and lack of application of conceptual teaching methodologies by teachers.[43]

The whitening of the African mind through imported models has proved to be a lamentable failure for the huge masses of people in Africa. The results have been experienced in the spiritual alienation being experienced today.

Spiritual experiences being witnessed today are partly dealing with these historical spiritual, economic, political and socio-cultural alienation of an African. It can be argued that colonial Christian evangelizations were and are prescribed consciously for domination and controlling of Africans.

However, what was and is not appreciated is the plurality of cultures in Africa and their different approaches to life, be it political, economic, religious social and cultural. It is like prescribing the same type of medicine for different illnesses.

All what has been mentioned above brought together have not taken into consideration of an "African world - view", which gives meaning to a particular group of people. Each cultural group of people has its own way of looking at its own world and makes its own interpretations. It is a discourse of how the different realms of culture come together into a unified whole.

---

[43] Luckson, Saka, "Zambia's Education System: In the grip of a quality crisis?" fizambia.com. Accessed on 22.02.2021.

In this discourse the terms "world-view" and "cosmology" will be used interchangeably, for they mean the same thing. Both refer to a system of ideas and beliefs about how the world is structured, how the universe functions, what kind of worlds exist (material and spiritual), and how they are related to each other. People perceive human life and order through the specks of these worlds.

Religious experience for an African like in other religions is partly a human activity and a cultural construction. It is considered a cultural construction because religious experiences are partly built on what particular culture informs its people.

Some of the cultural elements find their origins in human experiences. These experiences construct a culture. Culture plays an important role in the spiritual experiences of the people.

It can even be argued further by saying that religious experiences are interpreted within a given culture, be it Christian culture, Islamic or African. Only that African religious experience is intertwined and interwoven with all aspects of human life by the force of the soul of African world-view. Religion for an African is fundamental, perhaps the most important aspect that influences life. It percolates every aspect of the life of the Africans and cannot be studied in isolation.

For an African it is not enough to depend on science, expertise, skills and merits of an individual capacity. These have to be complimented by religious and spiritual backing. Some and many events, circumstances and happenings are believed to be under the direction of spiritual influence and forces.

Many life events and circumstances are attributed to some religious influence. Even political leadership, no matter how mediocre it may exhibit itself it is something attributed to some spiritual origin.

It is not surprising that General Ignatius Kutu Acheampong of Ghana showed his reliance on religion when he staged a coup d'état on January 13th 1972. He believed in the spiritual power of his friend businessman, Kohan Johnson, who was believed to have extraordinary spiritual powers over the success of the coup d'état. Johnson fought for the coup d'état on the spiritual level. In his own words the General said:

With effect from today, I have taken over the administration of this country. I have support, both spiritually and in men.[44]

The coup d'état was being carried out at different levels, spiritual as well as secular. At the spiritual level it was under the influence of the religious powers through Kohan Johnson as a religious leader with special powers. Therefore, there is no aspect of life that stands independent of others in African- life- world.[45] At another level it was being supported by people. Religious sense permeates the whole African life and no single element can be exhaustively studied and understood in isolation from the rest and devoid of metaphysical experience, be it natural, economical, socio-political, moral etc. For some this indicates that an African is a superstitious being who interprets everything and every event from a metaphysical point of view.

On the death for example, of Mwalimu Julius Kambarage Nyerere, former president of Tanzania certain natural phenomena was interpreted in the context of spiritual experiences from his hometown and village. There was unusual down pour of rains, two earth tremors, rocks that had been standing firm for years rolled down hill and a monkey (Mzimu or a Muunda) went wild in the streets and cried like a human being.

The unusual rains are believed to wash away the foot- steps of the Chief (Mwalimu Nyerere) for no one is supposed to see where the chief has stepped. All these symbolisms indicate that something extraordinary had happened (death of president Nyerere) in the community.[46] These natural phenomena are intertwined and interpreted in mystical and metaphysical ways. All these elements are intertwined and interwoven in a whole African universe by metaphysical and mystical inter-connectedness. This reality of inter-

---

[44] John S. Pobee, "Religion and Politics in Ghana, 1972 – 1978: Some case studies from the rule of General I K Acheampong", *Journal of Religion in Africa*, Vol. XVII, 1 (1987): 44 – 62.

[45] Harold W. Turner, "The Way Forward in the Religious Study of African Primal Religions", *Journal of Religion in Africa*, Vol. XII, 1 (1981): 1-15; Lesiba J. Teffo and Abraham P.J. Roux, "Metaphysical Thinking in Africa", *The African Philosophy Reader*, ed. Pieter H. Coetzee and Abraham P.J. Roux (New York: Routledge, 1998), 138.

[46] http://ippmedia.com/dailymail/1999/10/23/dailymail2.asp. Accessed on 13.05.2019.

connectedness of elements of African life has been observed by A. Dondeyne:

> The world is not a simple sum of events or of perfectly closed and self-sufficient entities, but a synthetic and total unity where everything holds together, where the parts need and support one another and are comprehensible only within the whole.[47]

This interconnectedness of elements as observed in African world-view is referred to by Nyamiti as a principle of "Metaphysical Continuity of all Beings" in which he sees an orderly solidarity and where everything has its place.[48] This is important to take into account when dealing with religious experiences in African context. Religion does not stand independently of other realms of life. Religious sense permeates all lifelines and human experiences. Religious sense acts as a lens of evaluating, analysing and interpreting events and situations.

Bujo on this aspect of religion in Africa considers African religion as being the heart of the traditional African society. This understanding of African religion will according to Bujo appreciate the theological context of Africa. Life in this case is considered as an undifferentiated whole.[49] All these come together and create the African world-view or cosmology. This makes an African a more religious being for there is nothing outside a religious experience. This is something very positive about an African when it comes to religious experience. Many life experiences have a strand of spirituality.

The African cosmos is a metaphysical cosmos. It is a world that is charged with spiritual energy (vital force) that holds everything together and into being. Death for an African therefore, is to be cut off from this energy of the cosmos. Social seclusion is considered as a spiritual seclusion. People who socially exclude themselves socially from others are considered enemies of cosmological energy and against free flow of life.

---

[47] A. Dondeyne, Foi Chretienne et Pansee Contemporaine (Paris, 1961), 115.

[48] Charles Nyamiti: "African Tradition and the Christian God" (Eldoret: Gaba Publications), *Spearhead*, No. 49, 59.

[49] Benezet Bujo, African Theology: In its Social Context (Nairobi: Pauline Publications Africa, 1992), 17-18.

This fact points to the extent to which the present fragmentary capitalistic society has harmed an African. Early Christian evangelization in many parts of Africa overlooked and disregarded this deeper and profound African spirituality. An African today is now searching for wholeness and to weave the society back into the cosmological energy of re-connecting everything into the whole.

On this score, an African already has a deeper understanding of how metaphysically connected is with the environment. An African has an understanding that uncontrolled exploitation of the physical and social environment can negatively impact on the life of an African.

The capitalistic fragmentation of society is not only in terms of economic inequality, physical poverty and lack but a spiritual fragmentation and emptiness. Spiritual fragmentation of the society is experienced in the fragmentation of human bodies manifested in some physical and spiritual illnesses.

Human bodies because of this disconnection from the cosmological energy, the bodies become spiritually vulnerable and may give way to be inhabited by foreign spiritual bodies that are strange and enslave the human bodies. It is a common phenomenon today to hear of men of God talking about a human body being inhabited by a spiritual snake, a wild animal, wild spirits, satanic and under- world figures.

This can create loss of social boundaries and to a certain extent loss of physical boundaries. Some people experience the loss of self in their own bodies. This is a feeling of not being in possession of one's body. They do not feel connected to something greater than themselves. They feel as people who are just hanging without being connected to something greater and powerful. Such people have a deep feeling of fragility and vulnerability from the outside world.

Rituals of re-connecting to the cosmological energy become very valued and important. This for many people points to the irrationality of African religion because there is some logic that is not understood from the point of view of an African. Western logic and philosophy cannot capture this reality because it is considered illogical and irrational in the context of western logic of practice.

A world-view therefore, is the lens used to observe the world and give meaning to the life of people. It forms the existential aspects of human life. It is the picture of the actuality of things, conception of nature, of selfhood, society and the comprehensive ideas of order.[50]

It includes the observable and unobservable, material and immaterial beings, the familiar and unfamiliar, the known and the unknown, the rational and the irrational, orthodox and unorthodox experiences.[51] That is why understanding magic and religion as operating independently becomes a challenge and a misplaced approach to African traditional religions. The realm of their expression is in the "whole". From this point of view, it can be argued that magic and religion share the same domain of the metaphysical level.

They both share an element of metaphysical aspect of the African world-view. Even today there is this modern anthropological postulation and continuity between magic and religion. In the case of African social context magic and religion operate in the same spiritual realm.[52]

Today it should not be considered as an old one out if certain aspects of traditional magic are being displayed in the present Christian religious experiences, for example, the claims of changing of water into paraffin by a pastor, the congregation lifting up their cell phones in the air and they receive phone credits (talk-time) from a man of God, becoming prosperous through the intervention of the divine gifts of men of God and giving more to receive more (sowing the seed). Other practices include the sweetening of the lives of the congregants with the anointed milk and honey as a method to chase away any danger that might do harm to the children of God.[53] Cultural and religious principles of these experiences are deeply entrenched in the spiritual lens of an African. Everything in African context is held by a religious strand and everything is held in a spiritual web.

---

[50] Clifford Geertz, The Interpretation of Cultures (London: Fontana Press, 1973), 127.

[51] John S. Mbiti, Introduction to African Religion (Nairobi: East Africa Education Publishers Ltd, 1990), 41.

[52] Cassirer Ernst, Lukay, Maureen, An Essay on Man: An Introduction to a Philosophy of Human culture (Humburg: F. Meiner, 2006 [1944]), 122-123.

[53] "Lusaka Prophet Introduces anointed milk and honey to sweeten lives of congregants", www. Zambianobserver.com/Lusaka-prophet-introduces-anointed-milk-and honey-to-sweeten-lives-of-congregants-2/. Accessed on 21.03.2019.

All these find their logic in the belief about African religion as permeating every aspect of human life. There is nothing that is outside the African religiosity. Religion sometimes may include the techniques of traditional beliefs.[54] Actually, some scholars have argued that the distinction between magic and religion is a product of cultural development of Western historical theory with its origin in Judeo-Christian concepts and concerns.[55]

Christianity separates spirituality from the secular, which is not the case with many African cultures. While this sense of secular and sacred is found in many African binary opposition concept (blessing/curse, sacred/secular, known/unknown.), but religion does not stand alone in contrast to other spheres of life.

All the spheres are intertwined into the whole. It can even be argued further that languages of many African traditional groupings do not have the term "religion" as conceptualized in the Western sense as an entity separate from the life of every day of an African. Religion for an African is in life as it is lived in every moment.

1.3. The Concept of Religion in Africa

Religion in Africa as a concept does not stand alone in African traditional religions. Religion is defined in the context of daily events and life. Religion in African tradition is something embedded in every activity of daily life. Even today, Africans living in the modern world still strongly believe in the existence of the invisible forces sharing deeply in the visible world and its events.

Religion is part of the people's politics, economics, health and sickness, social interactions, and every human activity. There is still strong belief that there are some modern institutions influenced and used by powers of darkness or the under-world. In the late 90s Zambia experienced some common spiritual experience in secondary schools and universities about Satanism.

This has led to the consolidation of prayer groups in compounds and healing ministries concerned with combating evil that operate in

---

[54] Ames Michael, "Buddha and the dancing Goblins: A theory of Magic and Religion", *American Anthropologist* (Hamilton: McMaster University Hamilton, 1964), 66, 75 -82

[55] Valeer Neckebrouck, "E.B. Tylor", (Leuven: Lecture, University of Leuven, 1999-2000).

modern institutions like universities other business entities.⁵⁶ Separation of religion from all life experiences is a Western approach to religion.

That is why, in Africa, religious rituals are performed at many given different times and events (personal, birth, puberty, marriage, death, agriculture, health, homestead, professional and festival rituals) because every event has a religious bearing on the individual and community.⁵⁷ Many moments of crisis call for the intervention of the divine. Some of the crises are created by change of lifestyle from traditional set-up to capitalistic environment.

Therefore, African traditional religions are very dynamic and it changes, accommodates, and domesticates new symbolisms, with time and social circumstances. It is not a religion that is cast in permanent norms and traditions like the Western Christian religion which does not change easily.

African traditional religions take into account new challenges and needs of the people. African traditional religions easily accommodate what is new. At the same time retains what is old if it is still relevant, useful and meaningful. It has some inner dynamism and capacity for continuity and innovations.⁵⁸

African traditional religions on this score can be considered more dynamic than the western Christian religion enshrined in norms, structures and dogmas that are cast in books.

African religion has no single and permanent ritual formulae to be followed by all ritual leaders. For a long time, there has been in existence some prejudices against the dynamism of African traditional religions, especially when Africans use the expression that *"this is what we have always been doing"*. For some and especially the Westerners this expression means that the African cosmology is static and that Africans resist change. However, it is observed that what people say and think about their religious representations, experiences and practice, on one hand and the real historical picture on the other hand may be different. The African religions are more pragmatic than just normative in nature. While Africans are fond of the expressions, "this is what we have always been doing; "we do this because this is the way our forefathers behaved", it can still be

---

⁵⁶ D.D. Kaniaki and Evangelist Mukendi, Snatched from Satan's claws, 38.
⁵⁷ John S. Mbiti, Introduction to African Religions, 131 – 143.
⁵⁸ Laura S. Grillo, "African Religions", Microsoft Encarta (DVD) Premium 2009 Redmond, (WA: Microsoft Corporation, 2008).

observed that African traditional religions have accommodated new symbols and representations in their expressions.[59] It is an expression of continuity and value but not in the dogmatic way.

The nature of African Traditional Religions is very open and accommodative as we are going to see later. This is what is being observed in many new churches in Zambia and their religious expressions and experiences.

There is continuity of the conceptualization of African traditional religions with a lot of accommodations from the present socio-cultural setting of capitalism and its symbolisms leading to a religion of prosperity and healing. This is a proper accommodation of symbolisms of capitalism. It is believed that a religious leader has the power to use spiritual powers to bring about economic change and better life in their followers.

Both in African traditional magic and religions, there is belief from the point of the agent that man has the ability to intervene in natural determinism to change the course of events. In nearly all religions there is this belief about change, transformation and spiritual shift.

Levi-Strauss on this point of view argues that there is no religion without magic or magic without a trace of religion.[60] On the contrary James George Frazer argues on the basis of dichotomy between magic and religion.

For him magic is considered to be a mistaken association of similar and contiguous ideas while religion is understood to be belief in powers superior to man which direct and control the course of nature and of human life.[61]

This dichotomy by Frazer may not apply in the context of African belief system. Magic and religion share the same realm of metaphysical world. From a western point of view these two aspects are dichotomous, magic and religion. However, I take the consideration of magic as a mistaken association to be very simplistic

---

[59] Jack, Goody and Ian Watt, "The Consequences of Literacy", *Comparative Studies in Society and History*, Vol. 5, No. 3 (April, 1963), 304 - 345; Robin, Horton, "On the Rationality of Conversion", *African Journal of the International African Institute*, Vol. 45, 3 (July 1975), 373 -399 and Vol. 45, 4 (October 1975), 373 - 399; Michael, Carrithers, Why Humans have cultures: Explaining Anthropology and Social Diversity (Oxford: Oxford University Press, 1992)

[60] Claude Levi-Strauss, The Savage Mind, (London: Weidenfeld and Nicolson, 1966), 221.

[61] James G. Frazer, The Golden Bough: A new abridgement (Oxford: Oxford University Press, 1994), 46.

in the approach to the context of African traditional religions. It is argued from the western approach when it comes to magic and religion.

Magic and religion from the western point of view are dichotomous. Their realms of operation are different. This is not the case with African traditional religions. They both operate in the same realm of the metaphysical. Belief in magic is an element that is part of African traditional religions and belief system.

In the case of African traditional religions, traditional magic and religion operate in the same mystical realm and belief, though traditional magic is not very central, meaning that magic is not the foundation of African traditional religion.

This same expression of traditional magic and religions in the same realm (belief) indicate that just as any other world religion such as Christianity, Islam, Hinduism, Buddhism, Judaism, Confucianism and Taoism, African traditional religion is not a pure religion.

They are all religions that have a human element in them. They are religions that embrace and are embedded in human history and experiences. For example, Islam is a religion that means "peace" but there is evidence in its history how it is entangled in violence against humanity. The same is true with Christianity which is embroiled in sexual abuses for years and other institutional abuses. Other religions have their own share of human imperfections as well.

If there is to be a reasonable understanding of why Zambia has the present spiritual and religious experiences as we have them today, with a lot of questions and contradictions, its elements of "reasonableness and unreasonableness", a proper understanding of spiritual and cultural building block, what they believe in and what under lies these scenarios need to be understood and unveiled.

May be what we are experiencing in the religious space today is not something new, but that it has just changed its logic of practice to give answers to the present spiritual quest in the Zambian capitalistic, modern and technological society and human life.

Can we say with certainty that some of the experiences Zambians are going through spiritually and religiously today, are too unreasonable compared to the past? Is there anything that can be called new from the perspective of cultural belief and values in the present situation? It appears that some happenings in Zambia and elsewhere in Africa, mushrooming of religious institutions, being formal or informal, spiritual experiences, dependence on religious leaders and ritual leaders – prophets and prophetess, unreasonable rituals (sometimes involving sexual and physical abuses, belief in religion of prosperity, miracles), and belief in satanic powers and Satanism lie deeply in what many Zambians believe in – the world-view and in the way these are interpreted.

This line of thought is not arguing that Zambia's belief systems involve physical abuses, unreasonableness and irrationality, but that these experiences should be contextualized within the interpretation that is carried by the world-view in order to understand these religious experiences and why people believe in what they believe.

Like Gramsci in his *Prison Notebook*, this discourse will argue that every religion is itself a composite of distinct and contradictory elements.[62] Contradictions are part of every religion and part of human life. In this case African religious approaches and experiences are not exceptions. They have their truths from within their reasonableness and irrationality. These are some of the peculiarities of religions in general.

1.4. Religion as a Peculiar Phenomenon

Among some of the peculiar phenomena we have in the world is religion. Meaning that religion is strange and inimitable thing among human beings. Religion is generally peculiar in many ways. According to Hill, religion is considered among the outstanding powers in the world when it comes to "organized effort", which according to him is the definition of "power".

Like schools, social media and newspapers, religion is capable of moulding public opinion with a purpose of changing the human conduct, character and behaviour.[63] The power of influence of religion is something to reckon with in human life and history.

Religion has influenced human history and life in profound and unprecedented ways at personal, group, society and global levels. Religion has power and authority of its own. It is generally believed and accepted that religions proclaim togetherness and brotherly love at the same time world history is littered with contexts in which religions have stood to justify all kinds of atrocities against different

---

[62] Antonio Gramsci, Prison Notebooks (1929 – 1935), 420.
[63] Napoleon Hill, The Law of Success (Mumbai: Magna Publishing Co. Ltd, 2010), 74.

races and cultures. Religions have been considered as catalysts for prejudices, racism.[64]

a. Reference to Empirically Unverifiable Realities

It is universally observed that religion sometimes refers to realities that are empirically unverifiable and not only in one circumstance but many circumstances. Some of the fundamentals of religions are not verifiable but held out of belief and trust.

That is why they are held as beliefs because they cannot be verified as in scientific verification. You believe because you trust and trust means you believe in something you cannot fully verify with certitude. If you can verify with certainty some truth, then you do not need to believe because the truth is clearly certain. That is why to believe in someone or something is to take a risk. Belief in this case comes from trust.

Therefore, all religions since they are founded on belief have some fundamental truths that cannot be verified and therefore, they are all systems of belief. From this perspective it can be argued that religion is irrational at some level because it is not based on justifiable and verifiable facts or on proven scientific findings. However, religious beliefs are rational because they are widely held and considered reasonable based on common sense and spiritual experiences.

Therefore, belief becomes rational if it can be justified and not every content of belief can be justified and proven. This makes it possible for a human being not to believe in some complete rational beliefs.[65] However, people still believe in these empirically unverifiable realities and not only sometimes but always and ready to do anything for believing in them.

b. Appealing to Deepest Human Passions and Emotions

Religion is capable of arousing deepest human passions for beauty and ugliness, deception and honesty, peace and violence in the name of religion. Some of the well-kept decorated with passion and protected public spaces in the world are religious spaces. Some of the

---

[64] Bart Duriez, Johnny R.J. Fontaine and Dirk Hutsebaut, "A further Elaboration of the Post-critical belief scale: Evidence for the Existence of Four Different Approaches to Religion in Flanders-Belgium", Psychologica Belgica, 40-3 (2000), 153-181.

[65] C. Jarvie, "Explaining Cargo Cults", *Rationality*, ed. Bryan Wilson (Oxford: Basil Blackwell, 1977), 51.

most artistic places we have in the world are religious spaces. People can spend millions of dollars to maintain these places. A good example is the burning of the Notre Dame Cathedral in Paris, France in April 2019. Even before the cost to repair the damage caused by the fire was estimated, people had started to make financial pledges in millions of dollars.

The burning of the Cathedral aroused the deepest passions in human beings. Of course, there is another argument about the importance of the Notre Dame cathedral as an embodiment of French history and culture apart from being a spiritual place.

Millions of Moslems travel to Mecca which is one of the most sacred places in the Islamic world for prayers every year and re-enforcing religious and spiritual identity. And every true Moslem has to visit this sacred place once in lifetime.

Some people are ready to sacrifice dearly for what are known as sacred places than for any other spaces. Millions of people (Jews, Moslems and Christians) travel from distant areas of the world every year to what is known as the Holy Land (Israel), the homeland of Jesus Christ, Abraham, Moses and the prophets of the Old Testament in the name of religion.

The visitations of these sacred places bring out the deepest human passions and emotions leading to personal transformation and conversion. This is something peculiar about religion and what it can do to human emotions.

People have fought wars, Jihads and other violent up-risings in the name of religion, people have travelled long distances from Zambia at huge costs to Nigeria, South Africa, and Kenya for the sake of religion to meet prophets, pastors for prayers.

Religion has built elaborate symbolic architectural wonders of the world. Individuals have been ready to make great sacrifices even the sacrifice of one's life (given their lives to the point of death – martyrdom, spent large sums of money and given up pleasures of life) for the sake of religion.

A good example in recent years is the breakaway movement from the Catholic Church, called Restoration of the Ten commandments of God, led by Credonia Mwerinda, Joseph Kibweetere and Bee Tait of Uganda, on 17th March 2000, when together with their members of about 780 and more people, men, women and children burnt themselves and perished in the fire because of religious apocalyptic beliefs.[66] This was done in the name of religion. We have had similar religious incidents in America and other parts of the world who have committed mass suicides in the name of religion. In the name of religion some people have led a secluded and challenging life in deserts, caves, forests and monasteries.

Human beings, their houses and physical business structures have been burnt down because of belief in magic allegations, based on belief in traditional magic, where it is believed to influence the lives of others in a negative way through some spiritual and invisible ways.

On many occasions you can see how deep emotions and passions are aroused to act in this way. Some of these appear irrational and unreasonable to human mind, though in the minds of many these are taken as truths and realities at a different level.[67] Therefore, religion in Africa when it comes to the spiritual experiences being exhibited of irrationality, abuses and manipulations are pointing to how far reaching religion appeals to the passions and emotional aspect of some African people. Nearly every religion has had a share of some appeals to passions and emotions in history.

In some instances, the observed contradictions and irrationality appear to be in the mind of the observer and not the participant. The contradiction might be a point that is latent on the part of the participant in social functionality.

c. Belief in Non-Natural Representations

Religions in some instances have believed in religious representations that are very peculiar and based on non-natural events and states, virgin births, reincarnations, encounters with angels, revelations, miraculous healings and visions. All religions on the fact of belief in non-natural representations have plenty of symbolisms of such kind.

At the same time African traditional beliefs have symbolisms which are peculiar and based on non-natural states like beings which are a combination of human and animal physicality, like the Mami Wata of Central and West Africa. This is a believed water deity, generally an extraordinarily beautiful woman depicted with a fish's

---

[66] Encyclopedia, https://www.encyclopedia.com/environment/environment-altmanacs-transcripts-and-maps/movement-restoration-ten-commandments-god. Accessed on 2.09.2019.

[67] Bryan Wilson, Religion in Sociological Perspective (Oxford: Oxford University Press, 1982), 32.

tail. She is believed to help her followers with unexpected riches. Her followers are believed to have sexual intercourse with her in the spiritual world.[68]

Today in Zambia there are some Christian religious leaders believed to be relying on this water deity who is believed to be very strongly and the source of riches, spiritual powers and prosperity. This is a rich and deep intercourse between religious traditional representations and beliefs. In Zambia there is belief in what is called "Ilomba". It is a snake like being capable of embodying a human being and treated as a human being.

This has mystical powers to bring good luck and health, prosperity, and protection. People believe certain human beings are at times able of transforming themselves into animals like crocodiles "ifibokolo", dogs, rats, owls among others, for certain ends.

Christianity as well in its peculiarity believes in virgin birth which from a rational point of view is unrealistic. Realistically a virgin cannot conceive under normal and reasonable circumstances without a combination of female and male sexual elements, but people believe in such religious representations.

From an African religious point of view African people believe in witches who can leave their bodies at night to go and do harm on others, engage in sexual intercourse with sleeping human beings, fly on banana leaves or cooking sticks. Some people are convinced that having sex intercourse with a religious leader in a context of a religious ritual can pave way and open the religious pools of fertility for conception in the case of barrenness.

There are reports of some cases were a religious leader washes the sins of the members of the congregation with soap, bleach, detergent and water or a religious leader makes the congregation eat grass as part of the religious ritual to realize what they desire to achieve in life.

One religious leader a pastor in Zambia brought into his church what he called, "anointed panties" for barren women in order to conceive if used continuously for a month.

Unmarried women can use the same "anointed panties" to find a suitable man to marry. The cost of an "anointed panties" was at 250 Zambian Kwacha, which is about 12.5 American Dollars.[69] Many

---

[68] Klaus E. Muller and Ute Ritz-Muller, Soul of Africa: Magical Rites and Traditions (Maxeville: Konemann, 2000), 490.

[69] Rekeni, Mahorn, Zambian News 365, "Ndola based Pastor speaks on why he brought anointed panties to church", December 29th, 2020.

women would fall for this ritual of an "anointed pant". All these fall in the realm of unrealism. The question is what makes people to be religiously deceived and sometimes for a long time irrationally? What makes human rationality to be blurred with deception if we can put it that way?

d. Interaction with other Human Spheres

Interaction of religion with other spheres of human life like material culture, human behaviour, value system, medical, morals and ethics is another point of peculiarity of religion. Religion interacts with family values, systems of human life organization with its own stand on contraception, sex before marriage, bringing up of children, marriage in regard to homosexuality and polygamy. Religion interacts with economics in its dictates on business ethics, labour and prosperity spirituality.

Initially, Calvinists believed that only a small minority, known as the elect, were destined for salvation and the rest were destined for damnation. Economic success in a person's life was seen as a sign that one is destined for salvation. Prosperity and salvation were interrelated. In this way capitalism pushes on the religion of prosperity as a sign and indication of salvation.[70] This is a proper interaction of religion and economics.

This influence is very much alive today in Christian spirituality of prosperity. At the same time religion interacts with law and politics in many ways. Religion has an influential interaction with the medical sphere in many ways about the understanding of human life, in relation to euthanasia, organ transplantation, determination of beginning and end of human life.[71]

In certain circumstances religion has made claims of healing incurable diseases and medical conditions through miraculous means – intervention of God through prayers and intercessions. This is not strange to African traditional religions. Nearly every aspect and sphere of human life in African setting is permeated with a religious strand. For an African there is no sphere of life that is devoid of religious spirit.

---

[70] Max Weber, The Protestant Ethic and the Spirit of Capitalism (London: George Allen and Unwin, 1904 – 1905).

[71] Bernard Haring, Medical Ethics (Middle green: St. Paul Publications, 1991). Bernard Haring in his work deals with different moral issues from a Christian morality point of view.

Another good example of religion interacting with other human spheres is its interaction with politics. Political revolutions have ensued based on religious beliefs and convictions. A good example is the 1979 Iranian revolution with a significance of Islam in it. On a global scale there are examples of how Islam has interacted with politics. We have states that are declared as Islamic states that function on the basis of Islamic religion. Some other countries are declared, Christian nations and Zambia is as an example. This is a bringing of politics and religion together.

1.5. Interaction between Religion and Politics in Zambia

In Zambia we have seen and experienced the alignment of politics with religion, though with some challenges and contradictions. Religion plays a vital role in defining politics in Zambia. Politicians play religion and religious leaders play politics to such an extent that Zambia has a ministry for religious affairs among the government ministries.

Politicians know and understand how religion in Zambia has influenced politics before, after independence up to today. Political elites sometimes have been uneasy when religious leaders get involved in politics which is perceived as a danger to national unity and stability of government. Religion in Zambia has always played some influential role in political, social and economic life among Zambians.

This can be attested to from the historical point of view about the clashes that took place between the African Watchtower and the political establishment in the early 70s and between the Lumpa Church and the government in the late 60s. These two experiences stand as landmark examples of relationship between political elites and religion in Zambia.[72] Zambian memory is still fresh about how religion played a role in transforming Zambia from one party system to multi-party in 1991.

Religious leaders, usually with political influence and popularity, are co-opted into politics for government to silence them and have control over them and the populace. Religious prophetic voice finds

---

[72] Win van Binsbergen, Religious Innovation and political conflict in Zambia (The Lumpa rising), http://www.geocites.com/africanreligion/lumpa0.htm. Accessed on 25.02.2001.

its entrenchment in the cultural depth of Zambia where there is no demarcation between politics and religion as separate entities.

Politics and religion in African traditions cannot easily be compartmentalized. In many African traditions traditional leaders have always been symbolic leaders in relation politics, religion and economics.

Zambia is a good example of a country in which Christian nation notion is enshrined in the national constitution though the debate for and against constitutionalizing religion continues to rage on.

Some see it as a violation of separation between politics and religion while others perceive it as a source of blessings from God for the country. This is a desire that Christian imperatives may influence every aspect of the nation.

The Christian values to become part of the governance system of the country. At the same time putting the country to be under the guidance and blessings of God. This resonates very well with the people of Zambia because that is what African people believe. There should not be demarcations among the spheres of life, social, political, economic, cultural and religion.

Actually, religion is greater than anything. This is bringing together the invisible and the visible worlds into reality. Whether this is helpful or not, it is not the question. The issue is that one cannot separate religion from any sphere of African life.

The argument is that Zambians have always been religious people. The dualism and separation that sometimes is sort between religion and politics is a western innovation which is not a reality for Zambians.[73]

Contestation of this marriage between politics and religion has continued for a long time in Zambia. Some interpret this marriage as a political ploy to manipulate power of religion for control of the masses by the political elite. The declaration of Zambia as a Christian nation means nothing in practical terms of life of people.

The social, political, moral corruption, high poverty and inequality levels are real concerns. To the political establishment the declaration of Zambia as a Christian nation is something desirable because it digs

---

[73] "The Declaration of Zambia as a Christian Nation", www.lusakatimes.com/2010/01/22/the-declaration-of-zambia-as-a-christian-nation-2/. Accessed on 16.10.2019.

deeper into the reality of cultural life of the Zambian people though it has very little to offer in practice.[74]

The one contribution that can be seen is its symbolic contradiction, segmentation of society with its accommodation of different churches to the extent of weakening the prophetic biblical voice. The other is that it acts as opium of the people. Political elites and pastors are busy amassing wealth while the masses are sent into over-night prayers, singing praise songs and long life fasting. Even those alleged to be extremely corrupt and have stolen from the masses take part in the prayers, praise singing and fasting.

Many people in Zambia believe things are better because of the political declaration of Zambia as a Christian nation. The declaration has never been translated into practical life for the country.

Besides Zambia being declared a Christian nation on 29th December, 1991, by the late president Chiluba Frederick, President Edgar Lungu has gone further by declaring 18th October of every year as a day of "National prayer, fasting and reconciliation". This day in Zambia is a public holiday to allow people to pray and fast for the country.

Whether these declarations are working or not for Zambia very few people ask such a question because it is a genius logic that has dug deep into the African belief system. This is a genius way of tapping into the African religious belief system and logic for political power galvanization and control.

Anyone who questions this intercourse between the state and religion is perceived as an enemy of the state, driven by the devil and a Satanist. This entrenchment of religion in every area of African life is so deep that it cannot be questioned- "something that goes without saying".

It is something taken for granted and partly hegemony. Such an approach to religion can make it manipulative and abusive in many ways, socially, economically, culturally and politically. Today religio-political prophesies by religious leaders have found a centre stage in Zambia and Africa in general. We hear of political life predictions

---

[74] Conrad Mbewe, "Zambia as a Christian Nation," www.conradmbewe.com/2011/12/zambia-as-christian-nation.html. Accessed on 17.10.2019.

coming from some religious leaders, men of God and prophets about political leadership, economy and life of people.[75]

One finds it difficult to see and decide where religion ends and politics begin and vice-versa. A political leader in many African traditional societies can act as a religious leader on behalf of the people at some level. A chief, for example, who is a political figure in many African traditional settings acts as a religious leader on behalf of his people. In many societies and its local traditional leadership in Africa, chiefs are considered to have some divine origin. In the body of the chief different worlds are brought together, the material and the metaphysical worlds. Traditional religious beliefs and practices underpin political power and political concerns have their basis in the heart of religion.[76]

It is evident today in Zambia that political elites make use and align themselves with religious communities for the purpose of mobilizing political support and organization of their political constituencies.

Huge financial contributions in form of cash and donations are made to religious groups and leaders to galvanize political support and populace.[77] It should not be underestimated that in Africa the spiritual world is considered as a resource for exploitation in religious and political life just like material, financial and military resources.[78]

---

[75] Predictions of electoral results some years away from elections, illnesses and deaths of political players. At the beginning of 2020 we have heard political predictions by Pastors, Prophets and men of God more than before.

[76] Tresphor Mutale, Zambian Democracy Betrayed: Patrimonial Corruption in Zambia (Ndola: Mission Press, 2008), 36 – 39; Stephen Ellis and Gerrie ter Haar, "Politics and African Religious Traditions", *The Journal of Modern African Studies*, Vol. 36, No. 2 (June, 1998), 175-201.

[77] This is a description of some "cannibalization" between politics and religion. Politicians dig their teeth into religion for political support while religion does the same into politics for financial support. This is true, how we have seen political and religious leaders becoming bed-fellows. Some religious leaders are so mute on the political corruption and criminalization of the state in the name of separation between religion and politics (church and state) that does not exist in Africa. The simple reason being they have "cannibalized" on political resources through financial gifts from politicians – "ukubalishamo" or "ukuswamo". These are Zambian local popular terms, meaning "having a stake in something".

[78] Jean-Francois Bayart, Stephen Ellis and Beatrice Hibou, "From Kleptocracy to the felonious state?" *The Criminalization of the State in Africa*, ed. Jean-Francois Bayart, Stephen Ellis and Beatrice Hibou (Oxford: James Currey, 1999), 21.

This is the metaphysical intercourse between religion and politics as we experience it in Zambia. During the period of fighting for independence some religious movements often carried an anti-colonial political tone in contrast to being religious alone. They were partly protest movements against western Christianity and as a cultural renaissance to the imperialism of colonization.[79]

In Zambian local politics, some politicians consult people known as prophets, Seers, men of God and medicine men for political success in winning elections and people's support against opponents and getting political positions. Some religious leaders are looked at as having the spiritual capacity to influence the way people cast their vote. Rationally this is impossible and unproven. The fact that people believe in these empirically unverifiable realities demands for an explanation and not just mere condemnation.[80] Sometimes we believe these can be taken care of by stringent laws to punish participants. This does not change the world-view in short term. This sometimes just pushes the beliefs to the underground from the surface just as Christianity did with traditional beliefs during its early evangelizing project.

Christianity and its missionaries believed that they had overcome the beliefs of the pagans through, new belief system, legal, suppression of local customs and social sanctions. There is no doubt today that people still believe and appeal to their traditional practices that are contrary to Christianity and Western logic.

Christianity condemned some of the traditional practices of the local people with ex-communications, other exclusions and punishments. What happened was that the newly converted went back to the same condemned practices in secret. And this still goes on today.

Many Christians still go out to seek help from diviners, prophets, witch-finders, cults, among others, when they are faced with a crisis, especially if it persists without any explanation. Therefore,

---

[79] Here the movement for Alice Lenshina (Lumpa Church) is a very good example. Her movement was both concerned with socio-cultural and religio-reforms for independent Zambia.

[80] Pascal Boyer, The Naturalness of Religious Ideas: A Cognitive Theory of Religion (Berkeley: University of California Press, 1994), 48; Walter Burkert, The Creation of the Sacred: Tracks of Biology in Early Religions (Cambridge: Mass, 1996), 142 – 143.

condemnation alone does not necessarily change the world-view and give solutions to aspirations and needs of the people.

An African seeks answers and meaningfulness of life. And what is held and believed in from the world-view gives solutions, explanations and answers to life as it is lived.

We can argue therefore, that even the spiritual and religious experiences and happenings in Zambia today are embedded in the religious traditional lenses used to look at the world to interpret life experiences, either positive or negative.

All these draw their persuasion from the world-view or the cosmology. Sometimes it is easy to laugh at some members of local communities who are alleged to have been abused by religious leaders and other ritual leaders in different ways.

The question is, do we go deeper in the belief system to analyse why these members of the community offer themselves to such unreasonable, unverifiable and childish spiritual experiences? Is there any reasonableness underlying the unreasonableness and rationality underlying the irrationality? Definitely there should be something deeper but not observable at a glance!

1.6. Spiritual Power of Interconnectedness

Zambian world-view as part of the African world-view is based on the power of relationships which are both material and immaterial. Africans have a sense of unified reality of the experiential world. For an African divinity and humanity cannot be isolated. The sacred and the profane interact in the same way the body is united to the soul.

Divinity therefore, indwells the physical world. There is a spiritual intercourse between the visible and the invisible. All that exists in the invisible and visible worlds have influence over each other. The world of the spirits or the spiritual world participates in the human world. This makes the spiritual needs to be as important to the body just as the physical needs are to the body. This makes the idea of dualism not to have a place in African thought when it comes to religion and life.[81]

In African world-view taking care of one another in terms of material needs is something very important especially taking care of

---

[81] Chris Nwaka Egbulem, African Spirituality, 18.

the material needs of your own kins. Turning against your own kins in time of need is believed to bring about bad lack, curse and misfortunes. It is considered as cutting oneself from the source or cutting off from the life-line or umbilical code and the web of life.

This is the basis of extended family. These exchanges made through materiality are underlined with unseen interconnectedness and immateriality because of spiritual connectedness. Relationships and exchanges can enhance or can weaken a human being depending on situations and intentions.

Therefore, material exchanges have a spiritual orientation. Even a simple greeting has a spiritual undertone. A greeting has a spiritual strand between people. Deliberate ignoring of someone and not to give a greeting may be misinterpreted and can severe relationships. A greeting in an African context carries with it a spiritual connection to one another. It indicates a free flow and openness to life with the other.

Selfishness, extreme individualism and self- centeredness indicate something deeper and negative about a person in the context of African tradition and culture. A self-centred person is a person who is ready to disconnect from the flow of life and ready to kill the flow of life. There is no relationship that is neutral in an African context. A relationship may affect a person in a positive or negative way from the observable and unobservable points of view. That is from the material and spiritual points of view.

Therefore, relationships in Zambian context and Africa in general are very important aspects because they determine one's individual life, well-being and harmony of and with the community. Actually, in African context one cannot be without relating with others.

Relationships are lifelines of communication. Through relationships and exchanges life is passed from one person to another. These relationships have as well existents in the unobservable realm. To this belief, diseases and misfortunes are looked at as an indication of weaknesses and disruption in human relationships.

This in turn affects individuals in form of physical illnesses.[82] Physical illness is a symbol of something missing or gone wrong socially deep in the web of human relationships. Body weakness and

---

[82] Remy Beller, Life, Person and Community in Africa (Limuru: Pauline Publication, 2001), 38.

illness are a symbol of some underlying spiritual chaos and tension within the social surrounding or environment of a person.

A weak body points not only to the disintegration of the human body but to the disintegration and disruption of community life and relationships. Even traditional healing of the body takes a social orientation, involvement of others in order to reconnect the weaker body to the flow of life of the community. An individual human body is not only a physical body.

It is a social body as well. Healing of human bodies is therefore, physical, spiritual and social. Modern health institutions in this case only take care of the weaker physical body and not the spiritual and social aspects of healing. This is something which has never been considered by western medicalization in African.

Modern health facilities in this case become places of contradictions and places of nowhere. They are spaces of privacy but at the same time places of guessing and social intrusion by strangers who examine the physical bodies with machines and physical instruments. These are places that deal only with fragmentations of physical bodies and not human and social relationships, fears, spiritual disintegration, social ill health, social exclusion etc., which can drain human confidence, which find basis in spiritual illnesses.

A Modern health institution is a symbol of dichotomy between a medical physical body and a social body or spiritual body which in African traditions is inseparable. Traditional medicalization takes into account the whole person, bodily, relational and spiritual.

Healing in African context is considered as weaving the threads of spiritual life and not only centred on the physical body, which is a western approach to illness. Life of the human body and social life are interrelated and interconnected in African milieu.

Human relationships in African context fall under spiritual and religious logic. An African is just a part of the whole material and metaphysical realities that exist. Being in the world has to be considered in relation to other beings in material and immaterial form.

According to Nkemnkia, in his reflections, *African vitality*, argues to say, there is no space for dichotomies between matter and spirit, religious commitment and daily life, soul and body, the world of the living and the world of the dead.[83] There is no realm of life that stands independent of others in the case of African life.

If there is a disorder in the invisible world, this will have inevitable and negative effect on the physical fortunes of the community and individuals. There is a continuous flow of life back and forth between the two worlds through a spiritual strand or what we may term as a "spiritual umbilical code".

When this is blocked or suffocated it can lead to failures in human life of different forms and misfortunes. Blockades and suffocation can come from different causes. Reconnecting becomes very important for life through spiritual rituals. This belief points to the importance of celebration of rituals in African life context.

Every element is interrelated to other elements and to the whole. This helps to understand why some physical and spiritual experiences are related to other relational experiences. There is no experience that is devoid of relationship. Relationships play a vital role in daily experiences of life. We would therefore, in simple terms explain the African world-view as a "web of relationships".[84] This is where everything is interrelated to the other at a deeper level.

It is these deep spiritual structures of relationships that determine what is observable and experienced. These innate spiritual structures are more powerful than the observables.

These unobservable structures are the ultimate principles from which the real experiences and their meaning are deduced. It is these spiritual relationships of beings that define "being" in Bantu philosophy. These innate structures are liable for manipulations by personages with power to access them.

They can be enhanced and they can be abused in evil ways. Accordingly, magic, some religious experiences, witchcraft, sorcery, Satanism and today's prophetism are a negative manipulation of these deep spiritual structures that exist among relationships of African people.

Today's spirituality and religiosity in Africa and Zambia in particular are exploiting these beliefs to their own advantage. This has been turned into an economic resource or capital by those who

---

[83] Martin Nkafu Nkemnkia, African Vitality: A Step forward in African Thinking (Limuru: Pauline Publication, 1999), 9.
[84] Godwin S. Sogolo, The Concept of Cause in African Thought, in Pieter H. Coetzee and Abraham P.J. Roux, 182.

are believed to have power to tap into the web of life strands. Some can take this as causal explanation of religious experiences in Africa.

The causal explanation of religion explains religion in terms of non-religious factors as the ultimate explanation of religion. These may include biological, psychological economical explanations of religion.

This way of explaining religion looks at religion not as reality of its own but an expression of something socially constructed. While religion can be explained in those terms, it has to be pointed out that the objective of religion is the transcendent reality.

Therefore, it is beyond the reductionist approach by reducing it to economical and psychological reasons instead of symbolic and ritual approach. Through symbols and rituals, the sacred makes itself immanent. This is true for African traditional religions.

In fact, African society is known to be based on symbolic interactions like other societies. There are invisible structures that are deeply seated in these social interactions. Interactions in these relationships are pregnanted or embodied or packed with deeper meanings, it being negative or positive in nature. In this case therefore, what is observable from a scientific point of view is only a part of the greater reality of the unobservable for an African.

There is a continuous interaction of spiritual forces undying relationships of different kinds. One is capable of enhancing one's interaction with other unobservable forces for posterity and success. At the same time, one may as well protect oneself from annihilation and diminishment from the negative forces of manipulation.

That is why protection against undesirable forces is something to pay attention for an African. People to protect themselves can use different things and approaches both based on cultural traditions and Christian symbols. This is where Christian symbols like holy water, oil and other ritual symbols are domesticated to replace traditional and local cultural religious symbols.

1.7. Under the Physical Reality

One of the hall-marks of African traditional religions is the interaction between the visible and invisible realities. Reality for an African is not only what is provable and material. It includes metaphysical existents. Connected to the belief of interaction between the visible and invisible realities is the belief in the existence of invisible power or energy that can be tapped and trapped and disseminated to others for the good of the community or individuals.[85]

Therefore, an African is able to tap into this metaphysical world to use the forces for human good and personal interests. At the same time an African can tap into the metaphysical forces for evil ends and objectives. This is where the reality of witchcraft lies.

An African through the enhancement of personal force and energy can have influence on a court out- come, love life, behaviour of another person, human fertility, sexual life, even on material things like economic production and prosperity.

There are spiritual authorities that are believed to tap into these spiritual powers and energies to change the lives of people negatively or positively. These can find lost lovers, boosting businesses, finding employment, solving financial problems, pass examinations, promotion at work, help in criminal cases, winning big tenders and contracts, and casinos, winning lotto, competitive games and casting spells on other people. Today in Zambia some religious experiences are related to some of these needs.

According to Tempels, Africans are related not only by blood relationship but by a spiritual strand that connects everyone to the other. This is termed as the vital force. The vital force is the life of the soul of an African. It links the ancestors, the living and the material world.[86] To be in good health depends on the good relations existing among people, or between the individuals, the group, and the environment of the life-world.

It is the proper integration of life elements which also determines the fertility, health, prosperity, cohesion, harmony of the social group, successes and material well-being of persons.

That is why in many cases anti-social behaviours are believed to be the sources of witchcraft beliefs. This makes "Individualism" something that is considered inhuman in many African traditional settings. Anti-social behaviour is considered something against the free flow of life energy. This is where performance of rituals matters

---

[85] Damian Kanuma Musonda, "Theological Reflections on Inculturation" (Lusaka), http://www.jctr.org.zm/inculturation.htm. Accessed on 4.01.2001.

[86] Some scholars have referred this connectedness to what they call "vital force". Placid Tempels, Bantu Philosophy, ed. (Paris: Presence Africaine, 1969), 50-51; Albert G. Mosley, African Philosophy, (New Jersey: Prentice Hall, 1995), 62-67.

most. Rituals help to unblock the knots that prevent the free flow of life-giving energy.

In this case, physical bodily weaknesses and illnesses are mostly seen as symptoms of underlining spiritual illnesses which cannot be addressed only by modern medicalization.[87] Many illnesses are underlined with spiritual influences and interpretations.

This does not necessarily exclude knowledge and acknowledgement of the role of natural causes. But further fundamental questions in the mind of an African are asked. An explanation of a virus attack to the physical body of a person may be given. But questions which modern medicine does not ask will be brought into enquiry.

These questions lead on the path to social-mystical causal factors; why did the virus attack this person and now? This is a question that is the crux of the matter when it comes to explanation and interpretation of illnesses and misfortunes among Africans. Some people are very poor and some are very rich in the same community and society.

Economists can come up with reasons being lack of trickle-down economic policies and poor planning and mismanagement of natural resources. These are not the only reasons for failure to prosper. These may have been caused by some unseen spiritual principalities.

A medical expert may explain very well the existence of a virus that causes a certain disease leading to the death of a person, but the medical expert would not explain why it entered this particular person and at that particular time.

There are very good and rational reasons given by scientific experts. However, the question for some to be very rich and some to be very poor, some not dying by the same virus, some dying, is not adequately answered, but why me among very poor, why the virus attacking me and not the other person? This is a fundamental and metaphysical question that begs for an answer for an African.

This logic applies as well to natural disasters like floods, pestilence and droughts. The invisible world can play a part even in natural calamities. This year, 2019, Zambia has experienced some drought in the southern part of the country leading to drastic receding of water

---

[87] Clive, Dillon-Malone, "The Mutumwa Church of Peter Mulenga (Part II)", *Journal of Religion in Africa*, Vol. XVII, 1(1987), 2-31.

in the Kariba dam which is the source of much hydro-power generation for the country.

This has made the country to experience the waste electricity power outages. There is a cultural belief narrative that the spirit called Nyami Nyami (of the Tonga people) was infuriated at the construction of the dam in 1956 for it separated Nyami Nyami from his wife by the demarcation of the wall of the dam.

It is strongly believed that the construction of the dam had destroyed the spiritual habitants of this place; spirits that dwelt on the Zambezi River in peace as a couple. This spirit, Nyami Nyami is still angry since 1956 and hence the drastic receding of the waters of Kariba dam which was built on the Zambezi river.

There are people who are calling for the traditional ritual to appease Nyami Nyami for offending him by the construction of the dam.[88] To many local people of this area, this is not just a legend but a spiritual reality. Therefore, it is not only climate change that is at play, but also the spiritual world manifesting itself through climate change. The physical reality in this case is pointing to some deep spiritual reality.

This same spiritual reality applies to other areas of life in African context – the question of influence by the invisible world on the visible. It is this same question many Zambians want to be answered in times of life challenges. It is strongly believed that some illnesses and misfortunes have some social and spiritual aspects or undertones that need to be explained.

This logical thinking takes into consideration the web of spiritual relationships and their influence on everyday life. Some Illnesses and misfortunes are characterized and interpreted in terms of human-social relations and spiritual interactions.

Therefore, illnesses and bodily fragmentations are not only a medical issue but are social and spiritual issues as well.[89] This is why an African may approach a prophet, priest, diviner and at the same time approach a modern clinic or hospital, because illness has two dimensions; spiritual and physical.

---

[88] "The Legend of Nyami Nyami", https://victoriafalls24.com/blog/2014/03/21/the-legend-of-nyami-nyami. ; It is Nyami Nyami, not Climate Change. Accessed on 08.10.2019.

[89] Rijk van Dijk, Ria Reis and Marja Spierenburg (Lusaka: Book World, 2000), 62 – 63.

Illness is connected to two broader phenomena, that is, cosmological or religious forces and social relationships and interpersonal conflicts.[90]

What Devisch says about the Yaka people of Southwestern Democratic Republic of Congo (DRC) is true about many tribes in Zambia:

> Illness is considered not so much as a mere process in the body alone but as stemming from a disturbance in the relationship between persons and their life-world. Illness is not in the last instance considered to reside within the individual, but derives from some disturbance in the relationship between persons themselves and/or between them and the life-world.[91]

Therefore, among many Zambians many kinds of misfortunes, sufferings and eventually deaths may be interpreted and experienced as coming from outside forces that disturb and destroy relationships.

From the above, one does not get sick, become infertile, die in a road accident, have a poor crop harvest, go through difficulties, remain unmarried, unemployed, die suddenly, not prosper in business, get demoted at work from natural causes alone.

All these in many circumstances are believed to be caused by unseen or invisible forces. And all these do have a spiritual under tone. They are all spiritual experiences being played in the "web of spiritual relationships".[92]

1.8. Science and African Traditional Religions

There has been over a long time approaching the "other", who does not apply scientific principles and explanations to situations as being irrational. Reason is one of the human facets taken for granted as the yardstick of measuring reality by science.

Meaning that, human beings communicate with reality through rationality. Let us not forget that even Adolf Hitler in all that he did

---

[90] Robert A Hahn, Sickness and Healing: Anthropological perspective (London: Yale University Press, 1995), 24.

[91] Rene Devisch, Weaving the threads of life (Chicago: The University of Chicago Press, 1993), 17.

[92] Ela Jean-Marc, My Faith as an African (New York: Orbis Books, 1988), 50.

he was reasoning and he was rational through irrational acts against humanity.

Some scholars have termed this spiritual web of relationships about African life as "superstition" because it has no real basis in science or what they call "true religion" based on rationality.[93] Anything outside science and "true religion" was approached with scorn and superstition.

Science and Western religion became the yard-stick for normality and acceptability. What is "true religion", in this case? Popularly, and for a long time now traditional Christian teachings, of main line churches and exact sciences are taken as the yard-stick or criteria for the validity of such conclusions of superstition.

I would argue that reasoning is something that is universal. By this all human beings share in this universality of reason. It is the human reasoning that gives rise to different cultural logic and civilizations in various forms in different parts of the world in different historical context.

It has to be pointed out that the Western culture in Africa has been propelled by the basic alliance between Western science and Western Christianity. This is evident in the transmission of missionary evangelization through education in Africa. Western Christianity taught a new way of interpreting reality through the Christian bible and its doctrines.

At the same time its education included principles of science through biology, new languages, logic, philosophy and mathematics. This made Christianity as part of the grand civilizing project in Africa and many other parts of the world.[94]

In terms of religion, local and traditional settings were introduced to new concepts about God as omnipotent, transcendental, omnipresent, among others. Of course, some of these concepts described the God already known to the local people through simple, practical and down to earth concepts like *"shicaibumba"*- self created, *"ntumbanambo mutima kayebele"*- one who decides on His own and many more.

These are descriptive concepts about God. They characterize who the supreme-being is. However, the world of an African was seen,

---

[93] Charles, Nyamiti: "African Tradition and the Christian God", *Spearhead*, No. 49, 59. 9.

[94] Ali A. Mazrui, The African Condition: A political Diagnosis (Cambridge, Cambridge University Press, 1995), 50.

evaluated, analysed and judged through the newly introduced faith and its Theo-philosophical concepts. Christianity became a judge on the religious experiences of other people's traditional religions.

Anything that did not fall within the already tailored Christian religion was considered pagan and irreligious. Christianity became the criteria for judging other religions and beliefs. This has remained so to date.

The question is what makes science and traditional Christian religions the criteria for such conclusions? Does it mean that reality is that which is only concluded and proven by science and the Christian religion and anything outside science and Christian belief is not reality? For a long-time science and Christian traditional religions are seen as true determiners of reality. These are considered to be instruments and symbols of civilization and modernity. Through this approach great deal of local and traditional powers and authorities have been confiscated and usurped by science and Christian religion. It has to be pointed out that science and Christianity at some level are symbols of power and control over humanity.

For a long-time these symbols have been taken for granted without open contestation. Sometimes science and Christianity have taken advantage of humanity in the name of scientific conclusions and Christian beliefs respectively.

This has caused a tension and passive violence in faith between power from above and below, the centre and the periphery, rational and the irrational. Actually, there are a lot of Christian realities that are outside scientific proof, but they are considered as realities of faith.

And there are some realities that are outside the realm of intellectualist approach but which are realities at the level of phenomenology or through bodily experiences. This approach is based on lived experience of people and how the world is seen, perceived and experienced. These are based on the coding of thoughts in images and symbolic forms.[95]

Actually, this approach is held to have a greater promise for a more comprehensive and analysing of the totality of data concerning religious experiences, attitudes and behaviour.[96] Human reality is

---

[95] James W. Fernandez, "African Religious Movements", *Annual Review of Anthropology*, Vol.7 (1978), 195 - 234.

[96] Humphrey J. Fisher, "Conversion Reconsidered: Some Historical Aspects of Religious Conversion in Black Africa", *Africa*, XLIII, I (1973), 27 – 40.

understood, interpreted and explicated in various ways. Therefore, true meaning of some religious experiences should be decoded from within.

These can only be captured by human sensibilities and not only through epistemological principles and instruments of scientific methods. These experiences are beyond the purview of empirical science. This familiar position is supported by Evans-Pritchard and James Lett who recognize and posit that it is not easy to know the truth or falsity of religious thought.

Religious experiences sometimes defy the principles of science and traditional Christian normative teachings, doctrines and beliefs. Science cannot be the only instrument to prove whether certain life experiences are true or false. Sometimes and in many cases empirical epistemological procedures do not apply to supernatural phenomena.[97] By this discourse the argument is not that African traditional religions do not accommodate science. They do but a further question is begged for answers through African traditional religions. African life being permeated with religious strand, a scientific question is further probed with a religious question.

This means that under scientific explanations and causes there are religious explanations that are brought to the fore. This is the world of an African, it is a religious world very different from western and Christian world-views. From its point of view African world is rational and intelligible.

One from a Western point of view may explain for example, that one's business has gone under because of negative economic indicators of the general economy, poor business planning, strategies and indiscipline. For an African this is not enough explanation, for the "why question". The religious strand that runs through every aspect of life needs to be unveiled and explained how it has impacted on one's business.

It means scientific causes can be influenced by other hidden spiritual powers and forces. One may not be shocked to hear an African government minister or president calling upon people to pray over some calamity. People are invited to pray over the high prices of staple food in Zambia, maize meal.

---

[97] Evans-Pritchard, Theories of primitive religion (London: Oxford University Press, 1965), 17; James, Lett, "Science, Religion, and Anthropology", *Anthropology of Religion*, ed. Stephen D. Glazier (London: Praeger Publishers, 1999), 104.

Meanwhile, economists have already given economic reasons why the price of maize meal is high, drought, poor delivery of inputs, poor agricultural infrastructure, inconsistent agricultural policies, among others.

While there is acceptance of these economic reasons based on scientific findings, the explanation is complemented by religious reasons. This is not a rejection of science but science is re-enforced with religious belief.

In fact, science and Christian traditions are cultural bound to some great extent. Both emanate from specific cultural contexts, which like any other culture are partly human, imperfect and inexact.

The argument here is not that it is reifying African religiosity and spiritual experiences, but that African experiences have for a long time been judged and measured by other and foreign cultural bound instruments for certainty and proof. At the same time, we should not approach African and Zambian religious experiences in particular with simplistic western logic and minds.

It is important to look at why an African and a Zambian in particular behaves spiritually in the manner exhibited today and the logic behind such attitudes, beliefs, religious experiences and behaviours. This is what Christianity had missed in its initial project of conversion.

It approached and considered the African Traditional beliefs and practices with scorn, to such an extent that these attitudes are to this day still there in the approach of Christianity towards other religions, and African traditional religions in particular.

Christianity is more judgmental on anything that is different from it. Christianity is always missing the logic of practice of the local culture and people. Most of the rituals, initiation (born again), seasonal, marriage, name giving, cleansing, reconciliation, blessing, community building, for the dead, spirit possession, healing, that held the communities and societies together were disparaged and suppressed.

New rituals that had little meaning and very foreign to many minds of African people were introduced. This has been considered to be very fatal for the soul of Africa. The disruption of African life by Christianity went deep to the soul of African traditional religions. Now we have an African and an African world without a soul.

This has created a religious emptiness and a cultural spiritual alienation on a continental scale.[98] Will it be a wrong assumption to make that what we are seeing today in the religious experiences of Africans and Zambians in particular are a reaction to this cultural and religious emptiness and alienation in search for real and meaningful answers? Why is it that Christianity has never created a spiritual contentment in an African?

---

[98] Klaus and Ute, Soul of Africa: Magical Rites and Traditions, 442 - 445.

Chapter 2

Myths and Socio-Cultural Experiences in Zambia

According to Oxford English dictionary a "myth" is a story of seemingly historical event that serves to unfold part of the people's world-view in order to explain some practice, belief or natural phenomenon.

A myth in a symbolic way explains things as they are to give events and situations a deeper meaning and interpretation. Every myth contains some deep religious meaning not observable to the general and common sense perception. Myths have power to maintain, confirm and support social state of affairs.

Myths contain some fundamental information about the cosmology of people. They explain in symbols the origin, why things are the way they are, purpose and future direction of everything. They are a form of theoretical representations of reality and their essence.

Therefore, every myth has some value at a very deeper level. Zambia like any other society has had its own mythical experiences of religious nature. It is these experiences that have shaped the spiritual experience and realities of Zambian society as we have it today.

It can therefore, be argued that the religious and spiritual experiences we have today in Zambia have been built on what is deeply embedded and engrained in the world-view or African cosmology.

The African world –view at some deeper level has been shaping the religious experiences of today in Zambia. In this case, what only changes are the contents of myths and symbols that carry the meaning and interpretation of life from time to time depending on the changes that take place in the socio-cultural environment.

Contents of symbols and myths may change, but the world – view and its fundamentals still remain the same. In this discourse myths are a reference to representations that are symbolic in nature to explain reality as experienced by the people.[99] In the case of Zambia the underlining logic and rationality of most beliefs remain the same.

---

[99] James, F. Weiner, "Myth and Metaphor", *Companion Encyclopedia of Anthropology*, ed. Tim Ingold (London: Routledge, 1994), 591-92.

What only changes in this case are the symbols that take into account the changes that take place in the social and religious environments. Interpretation of events makes use of the available symbols present in the new cultural space or milieu.

Mythical experiences in Zambia have been very accommodative of new available symbols in order to make an interpretation of life. New symbols that have come because of modernity and change in cultural space are assimilated into the religious experiences in order to give meaning to the life-world.

As the cultural milieu changes, due to economical, technological and sociological changes, even the Spiritual environment changes. Due to changes in needs, cultural environment and aspirations of people, these changes take in new religious orientations and interpretations.

In the religious experiences, Zambia has lived through different historical and mythical experiences; the first is the experience of traditional witchcraft with its own symbolisms and a bearing on the interpretation of life. Witchcraft is one of the oldest mystical and spiritual phenomena in the world and particularly in Zambia.

People are born in it and die in it. This is coupled with belief in interaction between the physical and the spiritual worlds, spirits and spirit possession. These mythical experiences have had some impact on the interpretation of life at particular times in the life of the Zambian people.[100]

Robin Horton premised that changes in culture will eventually lead to changes in belief and world-view. A shift from the micro-cosmic into the macro-cosmic worlds and transformations that take place in society will change the belief systems of people.

This was believed that drastic changes will come with time and education. Local, specific and particular traditional beliefs will eventually diminish. Changes brought in by modernity will change the belief systems of society. People will shift from their traditional religions (micro-cosmic world) and enter into world and global religions (macrocosmic world). The world of spirits, that are local, will be taken over by the world of the Supreme Being.[101] It was taken

---

[100] Clive, Dillon-Malone, "The Mutumwa Church of Peter Mulenga (Part II)", *Journal of Religion in Africa*, Vol. XVII, 1 (1987), 2-31.

[101] Robin, Horton, "African Conversion, Africa", *Journal of the International African Institute*, Vol. 41, 2 (April 1971), 85 - 108; Robin, Horton, "On the

for granted that parochial and region, and tribal spirits will not be able to explain the global experiences and phenomena.

A macro-cosmic being has to explain the microcosmic experiences. Analysing the African societies today, all these have not died as purported by modernity but instead the local beliefs (microcosmic spirits) have been integrated into modern life and religious experiences at different levels.[102] Local beliefs have found their way into the beliefs of the global religions and modernity.

Today, the African religious experience is the opposite of Horton's argument. The breaking down of the micro-cosmic world has not only led people into belief in the world religions, but has shown the proliferation of appealing to local prophets, pastors, seers and local churches and beliefs.

These have enhanced and strengthened local and traditional beliefs. People gradually rediscover traditional religious practices which the Christian conversion had pushed into oblivion.

Interesting, Auguste Comte, one of the fathers of Sociology, believed in an unfounded belief that these traditional mythical stages will give way to the explanations by science. Meaning that what is explained through religious myths and representations will eventually be explained through scientific principles.

According to Comte, no metaphysical religious explanation will stand on the way of scientific knowledge. For Comte, the true religion will be finally in the subject of science.

This has not been the case. Science continues to explain its theories side by side with local traditional beliefs without contradictions. Both are taken as alternative explanations of African human realities from African point of view.

Christianity thought it would replace the African traditional religions through conversion. Existence of African traditional beliefs up to today point to something deeper about African traditional religions than what Horton, Comte and Christianity thought and projected. Not even scientific explanations will obliterate the African traditional beliefs. It has been recognized that the authority for example of non-western medical traditions is embedded in ritual practices which are part of the entire social order. This gives non-

---

Rationality of Conversion", *Journal of the International African Institute*, Vol. 45, 3 (July 1975), 219 – 235 and Vol. 45, 4, October 1975, 373 - 399.

[102] Hike, Behrend and Ute Luig (ed), Spirit Possession: Modernity and Power in Africa, (Oxford: James Currey, 1999), xv.

western approach to illnesses a great continuation in spite of the availability of the western medicines.

This is convincing in that we cannot talk about the withering and diminishing of non-western approaches to illnesses. Instead, we can talk about the emergence of medical pluralism or co-existence between local and global.[103]

2.1. Supernatural Myths in Zambia

At the present moment Zambia is grappling with a strong belief in Satanism, which has changed the religious landscape of Zambia. There are even other religious beliefs that have been accommodated at different times in the history of Zambia like *Ba Kamunyama*.[104] The stories of Ba Kamunyama during the 1940s and 1950s were widespread.

They were also believed to use certain specific vehicles (red in colour) for the purpose of raiding and operated at specific hours of the night. They would usually attack those who were drunk, lonely persons in the night and prostitutes who operated in the night.

There were widespread stories that certain fashions, ornaments and cosmetics for women contained Ba Kamunyama's mystical powers for initiating unsuspected victims into Ba Kamunyama figures and activities. Certain tinned foods were suspected to be flesh of human bodies under the guise of tinned meat.

These were all believed to be manufactured in the under-world and under the sea. This was proper accommodation of modernity (cars, cosmetics, new foods and articles of fashion) into the existing African traditional belief systems. Special spiritual powers were not only contained in traditional bodies like, nails, bones, wild animals, horns, night birds, among others. The two worlds, the spiritual and material were brought together into the religious experiences of the people. Symbols of modernity were turned into symbols and

---

[103] David, J., Hess, Science and Technology in Multicultural world (New York: Colombia University Press, 1995), 193.

[104] Bernhard Udelhoven, Satanism in Zambia: Touched by the Finger of Thomas (February 2008), 10-11. These are backup notes of the seminar. Bakamunyama stories were very strong between 1920s and 1950s. Bakamunyama were believed to be people who abducted innocent victims and extracted human blood by magical means. They later sold blood to Europeans for huge sums of money, who in turn used blood to make modern medicines.

instruments of traditional beliefs. This shows the dynamism of African traditional belief systems with ingenuity.

The under- world that exists in the spiritual realm is as real in reality as the visible world with its own hidden activities where the agents of evil plan and execute their malicious plans. Some of the human agents of the under-world are promoted to higher positions in the visible world of institutions and structure.

Even today, there exists some considered diabolic objects like, foods, perfumes, money and cloths sold in supermarkets believed to have been manufactured in what is known as "the underworld"- under the sea, mountains and rivers - the world of spirits with the intention of distorting and disrupting life in the visible world, by stealing, ritual killing and destroying life.[105]

All these were believed and still believed to be done for the sake of extracting life force, symbolized by blood and desire for money and getting rich.

These experiences are sources of panic in Zambian local communities. These beliefs have an economic, social and psychological impact. And all these draw their strength from the world-view of the Zambian people.

And this world-view has the power and ability to accommodate new symbols of modernity. Basically, Ba Kamunyama myths have their roots in the witchcraft beliefs in Zambia's cultural belief systems. Social life changes of 1940s and 50s had to accommodate the belief of traditional witchcraft in a new way with new socio-economic symbols like clothes, new food products, fashions and ornaments.

Mystical symbols of power are no longer only bones, traditional paraphernalia, other human and animal body parts or natural materiality. Modern objects can as well have a bearing on the mystical reality of African life.

---

[105] D.D. Kaniaki and Evangelist Mukendi, Snatched from Satan's claws, 39. Mukendi is a Congolese Evangelist and Prophet who is a testimony about the life of the under-world. He testifies that before converting to Christianity he lived a life of the under-world. And that the under-world is something real and it exists. Such testimonies have been supported by a Ghanaian preacher Rev. Ernest Pianim who is an administrator of a Christian Charismatic movement in Ghana. For him he talks about the proliferation of the antichrists under the guise of western institutions like the European Union – Ernest Pianim, Ghana in Prophecy, Kumasi, 1995.

It can be argued that Ba Kamunyama myths did not stand on their own independent of historical cultural beliefs. They were part of historical-cultural mythical landscape. These myths were re-enforced by the world-view of the Zambian people. This meant that the cultural belief system played a vital role in Ba Kamunyama belief influencing people's lives and interpretation of the world. When changes be it economic, social and cultural take place and bring with them disparities and difference among people an explanation is sort.

It should not be overlooked that during the 1940s it was part of the period of urbanization especially along the line of railway from Southern to the Copperbelt regions of Zambia.

Differentiations in socio-economic life of people and break down in cultural values started to be very apparent. Those who were coming into towns from traditional villages started to experience individualization, vulnerability, cultural insecurity and segmentation of community life.

There was emergence of social stratification, economic variations and disparities which brought about status changes in the new communities never experienced before.

All these threatened the people's experience of living in closed and unified African traditional communities. And an explanation was required to explain all these differences, contradictions, disenchantments, insecurities and disintegrations from a cosmological point of view.

Even the socio-economical, technological and cultural changes taking place today as instruments of connectivity and at the same time the fragmentations of society and individualizations are seeking answers and explanations. In such an environment people seek from their world view cultural instruments to help organize, interpret their everyday lives and create meaning.

Ba Kamunyama myth explained the life of people at the time and giving it a meaning from a physical and spiritual realities drawing from African traditional beliefs.

2.2. Witchcraft and Magical Myths

Magic in this discourse is used as a fundamental concept that includes beliefs and behaviours that are based on mystical connection rather than empirical or scientific approval. Magic manifests itself in rituals, spells, use of objects such as amulets and talismans.

Witchcraft here is a description of how human beings engage with magic. Therefore, witchcraft and magic relate to some encounters with the supernatural or attempts to control the supernatural.[106]

Some of the oldest social phenomena in the world and in African belief system in particular are religion, witchcraft and magic beliefs. They are as old as communities of human persons.

Human communities at different times in human history have dealt with the reality of witchcraft and magic in various ways. In the academic sphere these realities have been approached from different perspectives.

However, it has to be pointed out that magic in the context of African life is something complex. It ranges from what we would call traditional medicine to personal and collective rites of protection, productivity, fruitfulness, life with ancestors, cleansing, blessings and aggressive actions against others considered as witchcraft.

African magic and many African traditional beliefs definitely unsettled the earliest missionaries and colonial establishments and fascinated the explorers and travellers because these traditional beliefs became baffling, threat to European superiority of reason and theoretical thinking.

This was so because the practice of magic and African traditional religions would not obey and abide by the dictates of scientific notions, approval and logical thinking of the west.[107] Some of the earliest Western approaches to African traditional religions, witchcraft and magic still abound in the thinking of many people.

It has always been believed that these will soon be replaced by western belief system, religion and philosophies. However, this has not been the case as predicted a century ago by different scholars.

2.2.1. Bronislaw Malinowski on Mystical Beliefs

One of the known earliest western theoretical approaches to African traditional beliefs drew its application from functionalism with a well-known, social scholar in the name of Bronislaw Malinowski. For Malinowski he looks at magic as an element of culture in relation to other elements of life. Magic as part of culture

---

[106] Pamela A. Moro, Witchcraft, Sorcery, and Magic. Onlinelibrary.wiley.com. Accessed on, 05.03.2021.

[107] Johannes Fabian, Out of our Minds: Reason and Madness in the Exploration of Central Africa (London: University of California Press, 2000), 216 – 220.

is used as a tool for bringing about satisfaction for a particular human need. It is a way of responding to psychological needs, especially in times of anxiety and uncertainty, thereby giving relief and confidence to human beings.[108] According to Malinowski magic is an instrument serving human's biological and psychological needs.

Magic for Malinowski is a natural response where technical knowledge or control is inadequate.[109] Malinowski implies that, when technical and scientific knowledge fail to give an explanation, people are bound to apply other mystical means. Failure and lack of scientific methods to explain some reality leads to the application of magic.

It has to be however, pointed out that Malinowski projects the presence of scientific and western approaches in all societies since time immemorial. This is not the case. People in some societies, like Africa, came into contact with western and scientific approaches at some particular point in recent history.

Before this some societies still lived in their traditional beliefs which included witchcraft, traditional religions and magical beliefs. Therefore, it may not be entirely true to say that magic is applied were technical and scientific knowledge fails to give an answer or solution.

Malinowski's theory may be true in regard to Zambia's experience today where there are some interactions between African traditional beliefs and technical and scientific knowledge. There are instances were technical scientific knowledge is considered to have failed and people rush for an explanation from other non-technical and non-scientific instruments like diviners, prophets, witch-finders, and religion for explanations.

On some occasions both ways, traditional and scientific approaches are taken side-by-side and not because the other has failed to answer to human needs. Instead, they are used in a complementary way.

Local and state leadership during economic and social failures have appealed to religious and divine interventions (mystical way). National days of prayers and fasting have become common in Africa as moments of seeking solutions to monumental economic and social

---

[108] Bronislaw Malinowski, Coral Gardens and their magic: Soil Tilling and agriculture Rites in the Trobriand Islands (Bloomington: Indiana University Press, [1935] 1965); Bronislaw Malinowski, Magic, Science and Religion (Garden City, NY: Doubleday.

[109] Bronislaw Malinowski, "Anthropology", in *Encyclopedia Britannica*, (1926); Sex, Culture and Myth (London: R. Hart-Davis, 1963), 261.

challenges of society. A good example is the declaration of "coronavirus-free" Tanzania by President John Magufuli because of the power of prayer and fasting by the people of Tanzania.[110] Inadequate modern medical facilities, poor economies, household poverty and collapsed health care systems may serve as one reason for the thriving mystical approaches but not in all cases.

For example, it is general knowledge and scientifically proven and accepted that HIV has no cure at the moment once the virus enters the human body. Technical and scientific knowledge prove that. At the same time, there is strong belief that one can be cured of HIV through prayers and intervention of spiritual and mystical powers.

African societies have had some spiritual testimonies from people who claim to have been cured from HIV. Many of these claims have been sanctioned and medically certified to show conversion to being HIV negative. Some of these claims have been made by the late prophet T.B. Joshua.[111]

During the Cholera epidemic in Zambia in 2018 when many lives were lost, there was a call by government to have a day of prayer and fasting in order to have divine intervention.

This call pointed to a deeper belief that the cholera epidemic was not only social and medical in nature but a spiritual circumstance that called for spiritual intervention. This call, it should not be overlooked, it can be political as well. It can be used as a way of diverting the attention of the people from government responsibilities and social, environmental and health policy failures.

Many ordinary people will not see it as partly a failure of government health policies and political will but as a spiritual failure on the part of the people and as a nation which is declared a Christian nation. Therefore, spiritual intervention becomes more powerful than government policy interventions. African governments support

---

[110] BBC News, bbc.com, Coronavirus: John Magufuli declares Tanzania free of Covid 19. Accessed on, 16.01.2021. It has to be pointed however, that World Health Organization (WHO) is concerned about Tanzania's claim of being Covid 19 free country. It has baffled many people how a section of Tanzanians support the assertions of their president.

[111] Opendemocracy.net, Accepted mishaps? Faith healing, HIV and AIDS responses. Accessed on 04.03.2021. This approach of believing in the power of prayer to heal HIV is further exposed through a research in rural Tanzania, bmcpublichealth.biomedcentral.com, "Driving the devil away": qualitative insights into miraculous cures for AIDS in rural Tanzania ward. Accessed on 05.03.2021.

such approaches by encouraging religious institutions to hold such national prayers graced by politicians.

Between November 2019 and February 2020, Zambia experienced some ritual killings (spilling of blood) and gassing of homes by unknown people for unknown reasons during the night.

The report from the government investigations as to the cause of gassing and killing of innocent people is still being awaited. The government and the churches called for a day of prayer for God's intervention. There was a strong belief supported by the police service that when perpetrators were confronted in the night they turned into cats and disappeared.

This made it difficult for the police to make arrests.[112] Therefore, this terrorizing of communities was not only a social and physical phenomenon but spiritual as well. The African traditional belief was brought into play on the whole issue of gassing and ritual-killing.

Was this a failure of modern technology and skills of modern policing? It could as well be possible that the police were aware of the source of the syndicate of gassing as part of political destabilization from the top politicians, instead the police rushed into magic as a reason for their failure to make arrests.

However, magic has been part of African life for a long time. In African traditional beliefs, there is a belief that some people using traditional medicines and magic are able to transform themselves into other creatures and back again into their human nature.

It is true to say that sometimes it is the failure of modern technology, science, government policies and rule of law as known today to give an explanation which leads people to seek different ways of explaining reality. It should be noted and argued however, that mystical way is not a development that came from failure of technological approach and science.

People in Africa have believed and used the mystical approaches even before exposure to technology and science. Therefore, the mystical approach is not always the offshoot of failed technology. In this case a different explanation of persistence in this belief has to be sort and not only from the failure of science and technology. It goes beyond the failure of science and western technical knowledge.

---

[112] Zambiareports.com, Katanga Sheds Light on Chingola Ritual Killings, January 27, 2020. Accessed on, 25.01.2021.

Especially with the persistence of failure in health, misfortunes, calamities, unexplained sudden deaths, people look for some other means of explanation, seeking answers and fulfilling their desired needs. However, it has to be stated that, today the mystical way in the context of Africa and Zambia in particular should be approached as another alternative, independent of scientific approach.

African people in this case have considered traditional mystical ways not because of failure of technology as argued by Malinowski, but just as an alternative of belief in its power which is independent of failure of science. Sometimes, people after being admitted in hospital to receive western medical care, may secretly be taking traditional medicines combining the two medicalizations at the same time. How can this be explained today?

2.2.2. Sigmund Freud on Mystical Beliefs

Another earliest western approach to traditional belief in witchcraft and magic is the psychoanalysis approach by Sigmund Freud.[113] According to Freud magic finds its explanation in the unconscious and simply as a neurosis from what he calls the "world of fantasy".

As part of the world of fantasy, people who engage in magic, traditional beliefs and witchcraft believe and think that they can change the world around them by their incantations and charms. For Freud, magic is the oldest form of thinking and a normal functioning of the psychic processes at an early stage of human maturity. Psychic imposes itself on reality of things with a view of changing the same reality.

Therefore, excessive importance is given to thought. And he calls this "principle of the omnipotence of thought". Thinking that one can change reality by just thinking. It cannot be disputed that there are certain realities that can be changed by the power of the mind, but this is not in all cases. For Freud, magic involves just the use of the power of the mind. It means that magic and witchcraft are creations of infertile and immature minds.

For Freud therefore, belief in magic is the immature working of the mind and equates belief in magic to childish stage and a neurosis.

---

[113] Sigmund Freud, Totem and Taboo (London: George Routledge and Sons Ltd, 1919), 141 – 144.

Belief in magic and witchcraft is a form of human immaturity and some sort of sickness.

But can all the instances of magic and witchcraft be reduced to immaturity of persons and a neurosis? Is there no difference between neurosis and human immaturity?

Can we conclude that in this case the Zambian community is immature and neurotic to believe in this phenomenon of magic and witchcraft? This is where the challenge lies in applying the theory of Freud.

There could be some immature and neurotic cases surely, but not all cases. This is a simplistic approach to peoples' challenges and beliefs. The belief systems of people sometimes go beyond just the power of the mind or something psychological. Reality is not just in the mind. Reality may be physical and phenomenological.

It is common knowledge that cultures differ in their viewing of reality and behaviour that is reasonable and irrational. Here even the criteria of evidence, proof and truth may be different according to cultural context.[114] Sometimes a different kind of experience becomes necessary for understanding some reality. This position is not a denial of application of reason to understand the belief and actions of others.

Here we cannot take an extreme relativistic position that denies good reason from the bad one.[115] Reason has to be appreciated for what it is in human life but it is not the only way of understanding and knowing reality. Certain realities go beyond reason. Some religious experiences are as good as real, though not all.

Religious experiences go beyond social and bodily interconnections. They are able to help an individual to transcend the social and material world to bring unity between the physical, the social and the spiritual.

The person has an experience of the "return to the whole" through spiritual realm.[116] Sometimes reality may be experienced through the bodily experiences that go beyond physical phenomenon. Some human bodies have the ability and capacity to

---

[114] Gilbert Lewis, "Magic, Religion and the Rationality of belief", in Tim, Ingold, 581.

[115] Hollis M., Models of Man, (Cambridge: Cambridge University Press, 1977), 126-7.

[116] James Fernandez, "The Mission of metaphor in expressive culture", Current anthropology, (1974) 15 (2): 119 – 45.

embody some spiritual inner structures that can communicate to the outer world. I believe this is a case with some spiritual experiences among Zambians today.

In these experiences there are some spiritual realities beyond what can be seen and touched. Can we therefore, conclude with Freud that Zambian religious belief is a working of the mind or a mere neurosis? Does this point to the sickness of society and its people who believe in these spiritual experiences?

Are Zambians suffering from what we can term as a "national neurosis" and therefore, not rational in their belief? Or there is some rationality that need to be understood and appreciated beyond these spiritual experiences? Not all beliefs are the workings of the mind. Some experiences in all religions including African traditional religions are beyond human reason.

The reality in these experiences cannot be captured through the human mind. Mystical experiences therefore, cannot be reduced to a psychological welfare. Of course, this does not deny the role of psychology in mystical beliefs. Sometimes the society reduces the spiritual experiences of people to some psychological working.

2.2.3. Edward Burnett Tylor on Mystical Beliefs

Other approaches to magic and mystical beliefs include intellectualism propounded by Edward Burnett Tylor.[117] As for Tylor, people believe and perform magical actions because they believe them to be a means of bringing about ends which they desire.

This is done through the principle of association of ideas which a scientist does not do to bring about conclusions on reality. A magician postulates a causal connection between things classified by resemblance and contiguity.

Magic or witchcraft is failure to distinguish between associations of ideas made mentally and casual connections between things in the real world.[118] Tylor considers application of such principles, associations and knowledge to be erroneous and a big mistake.

Magic, according to Tylor, simply provides an alternative explanation value of some human events such as death, misfortune and illness on which human intellect would like to get answers but in

---

[117] Edward Burnett, Tylor, Researches into the Early History of Mankind and the development of civilization, 3rded. (London: John Murray 1878).

[118] Edward Burnett, Tylor, Researches into the Early History of Mankind and the development of civilization, 130.

a wrong way and big mistakes. This is the basis of the intellectual approach to witchcraft and magic.

It is true to say there could be many explanations of reality according to human mind. But are all associations in cases of magic and witchcraft erroneous? Meaning that they are all wrong and big mistakes in all cases?

It is true for all societies to seek explanations on challenging events in human life, like failure of business, unfortunate loss of a beloved one, sickness and others but are all instances of finding explanation in witchcraft and magic wrong?

What about confessions and testimonies given by some people considered as perpetrators of witchcraft and magic, should they be completely dismissed as misplaced and irrational? Of course, the environment of these confessions and testimonies need to be objectively tasted, analysed and evaluated with a critical mind.

Some of these have been made under duress or fear of death and torture. Some of those who practice mystical activities confess to pastors, men of God and priests. Some are just made voluntarily without any cohesion or attention seeking. How can this be explained? Is it attention seeking as some may put it?

All these have been attempts to give meaning to the reality of witchcraft and magic. Some explanation attempts have been made to dismiss magic, Satanism, cultic rituals and witchcraft as completely irrational not to be entertained in a civilized world and with developments in science they will fall away because science will give answers to all the questions raised by irrational minds.

This has not been the case in some societies like Zambia in particular. In spite of developments in science, technology and scientific explanations, people still adhere to the beliefs in spiritual-magical powers. People still believe in the power of witchcraft, magic, prophetic powers, spiritual intervention and Satanism today. This phenomenon continues to impact on local communities, domestic homes and life of families today. Witchcraft has continued to be a great tyranny which spreads panic and death.[119]

Advanced technology, education and civilization have not answered all the questions raised by life situations in times of misfortune, unexplained painful events and circumstances.

---

[119] Geoffrey E. Parrinder, Witchcraft: European and African (London: Faber, 1963), 9.

Many Zambians are still seeking answers not from science or civilization which surround them, but from people with "knowledge" in magic, witchcraft and other divine experiences. These knowledgeable people today in Zambia include Diviners, Witchfinders, Prophets, Prophetesses, Seers, Pastors and Religious leaders who are able to see what others cannot see and tap into the supernatural powers to give answers and explanations to human events and experiences.[120] Some religious leaders today are able to see the future events to be fallen on societies and individuals.

A traditional diviner is one of the most disparaged and persecuted ritual leaders by missionaries in Africa for the possession of local and mysterious knowledge. A traditional diviner still today is considered by many Christians as an embodiment of evil and representation of African superstitions and paganism.

On the contrary, for an African a diviner is seen as an exacting figure which has a concrete understanding of human conflicts in human relations, families and society. A diviner understands well the anxieties and tensions that arise from the religious realm among people.

A diviner decodes reality from the life experiences of the people. The fact is that not all explanations of reality fall under science and technology and not all explanations of reality fall under supernatural. This is the complexity of human life. Both these approaches need to accept their limitations.

The only new evidence of change of belief in supernatural causes is the way belief in witchcraft and magic have been accommodated in the new way in the newly civilized and modern environment and the approaches used to fight it which are now open to public observation and participation. It is a common practice today in both traditional and new Christian churches to find something very close to cultural and traditional divination as found in African traditional religions.

---

[120] Kate Crehan, The Fractured Community: Landscapes of Power and Gender in Rural Zambia (London: University of California Press, 1997), 189. It is now a common phenomenon by pastors and men of God predicting the future for people, communities and families. One prominent African pastor is able to predict illnesses of and eventual deaths of prominent people in society. Diviners in Africa are able to do the same. The difference is that diviners use local traditional material instruments to decode information while the pastors and men of God claim just to pass on that which they see and hear in the name of Jesus through visions.

Just like a traditional diviner some modern priests, pastors, prophets and seers have the sense of sniffing the source of a misfortune, sickness or an evil event. But since this is done in the context and boundaries of Christianity very few questions are raised.

Some religious leaders are expressing and practicing their Christian ministries just like traditional diviners. Like a diviner they will pin-point the source of evil afflicting the individuals, families and personal businesses. This is very interesting to an African mind for it comes in to answer the African fundamental question, "why?"

This gives a firm ground to argue that the general explanations and discourses given above from Malinowski, Freud and Tylor on witchcraft and magic do not apply to all human societies and at all times.

2.3. Belief in Witchcraft and Traditional Magic in Zambia

Explanations for how each given society, has dealt and deals with phenomena of witchcraft, traditional beliefs and magic has to come from within. The belief in magic and witchcraft is an existential question which can be encountered in many different ways among others like in the dreams and challenges of African context.

What is arguable is the conclusion that Africans are throwing themselves in desperation into mystical movements and religious practices because of worsening living conditions as purported by Ela.[121] In short, according to Ela, we are seeing and experiencing some extraordinary spiritual and religious experiences because of the adverse change in social life of the people.

Failure of people to cope with complex society and social challenges is pushing many people to fall on religious experiences. The truth of the matter is that Africans have lived in mystical circumstances even way back before coming in of modernity, organized economy and technological developments.

Africans have not come to believe in religious experiences outside Christianity because of social crisis. It is something entrenched in the world-view or cosmology.

It is something that is part of African life and belief. It is a belief about some spirits, natural and human and people's ability to cause harm to others, crops, animals, and even natural environment. It is

---

[121] Ela Jean-Marc, My Faith as an African, 119.

an innate quality which can be passed on from one family member to another and from generation to generation.

Witchcraft can be practiced unconsciously and in secret. It is considered a life in reverse and anti-social. Witches are social elements that are at odds with society values of solidarity, care for individuals and community life.

Their intention is always evil. It is an acting against one's human nature. It is a life that crosses bodily, social, physical and spiritual boundaries and with no respect for society norms.

There is a myriad of activities associated with witchcraft. Witches become active in the night than in the daytime, nakedness is preferable, flying instead of walking, incest and other forbidden sexual acts, they feed on human flesh, and witches would harm even their closest relatives.

Witches through magic manipulate the cosmic energy, which is the vital force (organic life force, power of nature and spiritual power) to influence, change and destroy through spells and rituals.

Witchcraft and magic beliefs in Zambia are embedded in the cultural belief system which draws its strength from the African world –view as exposed above. Witchcraft and magic are not engaged in for their own sake, but for what they can give the practitioner and the client.

It is believed that it can change one's circumstance by making use of mystical and metaphysical powers. Witches can use human parts of the body, even a shadow or footprints for their potency in business, in the production of high yields in the fields, bringing about certain events, influencing life of the individuals and communities and in many other areas.

I remember very well one incidence at one of the Boys' Secondary Schools in one of the big cities in Zambia in the early 1980s. There was a suspicion about one of the boys who was doing exceptionally well in class in form three that time. A word started going round among classmates that he uses witchcraft or magic during examinations.

He used to put on a small steel wrist bracelet which was alleged to be his fetish. It was believed that during examinations you should not allow him to pass behind you. If he did, he was able to take away all that you had studied and use them for his own advantage.

One day during examination time he was approached by his classmates with the intention to break the small wrist bracelet from his wrist. That was done. After sitting for the examinations, his results were as usual exceptionally good. Later on, it was discovered that he was given the same small wrist bracelet by his childhood girlfriend as a sign of their love.

This was for others an outright allegation of using magic in passing examinations. This one, experience of course, cannot help dismiss other experiences of belief in magic and witchcraft in the minds of many African people.

Witches in Zambian context are believed to fly at night. They have the ability to change into animals[122], become invisible and can kill at a distance. Actually, there is no place to hide from witches if you become the target. Just as other spiritual beings are present in the spiritual world, even the witches exist in the same realm.

And sometimes witches are able to use natural phenomenon like lightening, common illnesses like malaria, motor vehicle accidents, coughs, headaches and other illnesses in order to fulfil their malicious and evil intentions.[123] Even today and in this age, some instances of lack of success, failure in examinations, inability to gain promotion in office, some strange disease, lack of personal progress and especially barrenness in women and impotence in men are usually attributed to witchcraft influence.

Witches are believed to have ability to inflict untimely death, disease and material loss on others. They can make people infertile, impotent by destroying spiritually the reproductive organs and have the ability of making love to women in their sleep unconsciously. In certain circumstances witches are believed to feed on human blood and flesh as their source of food and nourishment to enhance their powers.[124] Ritual killings fall under this aspect of belief.

---

[122] Peter Kalumba Chishala, popularly known as "Professor P.K. Chishala" in the late 80s sung a song known as "Church Elder". It was a mythical song that spoke to the life experiences of many Zambians. Professor tapped deep into the belief of the Zambian society through the song. It became a very popular song played in homes, bars and shops because of its satire nature and went deep into some local beliefs.

[123] Bernhard, Satanism in Zambia: Touched by the finger of Thomas, 16-17.

[124] Bus accidents that have rocked the Zambian roads in recent years are interpreted by some people as spiritual activities of Satanism. The blood spilled in these accidents is for enhancement of satanic powers for business successes. And now prayers and preaching in buses for safe travel before starting off have become common for divine intervention.

At the same time human blood is believed to be used as fuel for nocturnal travels and human flesh as meat for food. Witches can make some acts in an inhuman and antisocial ways without one being conscious.

Witches in African societies are believed to have the ability to steal money wherever it is hidden and maize meal from homes of people and transform into animals or little human beings that can transcend any human boundary – "utumbuma" like snakes, crocodiles, hyenas, birds, lions etc.[125]

Today in some of the healing sessions in some churches, behaviours of the spiritually possessed persons manifest some animal like antics in sound and physical behaviour, crawling like snakes and making sounds like wild animals.

This is related to Satanism and working of evil spirits. However, this is a phenomenon that has been in existence for such a long time. Such an environment has made holy water and anointing oil to be popular and sort after by many people.

As I present this discourse, with the help of the Catholic community, we are taking care of an old woman who it has been alleged is a witch in the family and her community. It is believed that she has been behind the so many deaths experienced in her family including deaths of some of her own children. She has been neglected by her family members including her own blood children for fear of being bewitched.

At first even some Christians in her community (Catholics) believed the same about this old woman, that she is a witch but have since changed their position of belief about the old woman – that she is not a witch. I had to force them to look after her and care for her in her daily needs. All her relatives have vowed to have nothing to do with her. They are just waiting for her death. I have talked to the old woman at a very deeper level to find out if there is something about her pointing to those allegations. I have found nothing. I have tried to find out from one of the grand sons who was brought up by the same old woman, but he says he believes strongly that the woman is not a witch. Even the grand son has since stopped visiting her for fear of being ostracized by his family members.

---

[125] Joseph M. Hopkins, "Theological Students and witchcraft beliefs", *Journal of Religion in Africa*, (1980), XI, (1), 56 – 65.

The other hidden issue is that there is some power play over her ownership of the house behind the scenes which had compounded this case. The old woman owns a house on which interests have arisen over the years from her daughters. The old woman did not want and she has vowed not to move out of her house.

Could this be the cause of all these allegations about her to let go her house or the allegations are genuine and different and independent from her property, the house in this case? This life story is not a vindication of witchcraft shrouded in the power play over the property. The two issues may just not be related, that is, witchcraft and property.

But it cannot be ruled out completely. Sometimes issues of witchcraft come into play because of power struggles, fear, personal interests and jealousy behind the scenes of people in the social arena. However, witchcraft cannot be reduced only to a psychological fact.

It will be interesting to make a follow up on the life of this family over the years to see whether there will be different interpretations of deaths in their family after the old lady has since passed on. Usually what happens is that another person within the family will be taken on as a witch after the death of an alleged witch. So, the cycle continues.

Witchcraft allegations do not come to an end after the death of one witch in the family. I believe this is because of the influence of the world-view. Even after the death of the alleged witch, the family will still seek explanations of deaths in the family as long as deaths and misfortunes occur.

This is how deep the Zambian society is entrenched in belief of witchcraft and magic. With this one instance of allegation which is difficult to prove, I am not disputing the existence of witchcraft and magic in general. Witchcraft is a reality in African set-up and life experiences.

It is capable of influencing behaviours, social life, human relationships, beliefs, community structuring and balance of power. Witchcraft in many African traditional religious thinking has a theological position, for it answers the big question of "why", hence it serves an explanatory function and it is the same with traditional myths.

Witchcraft or magical practices are believed that they can be passed on from one person to another person through inheritance of certain objects like amulets, cloth, pot, artistic objects, human and animal body parts and many other instruments of this nature.[126] Others believe that witchcraft can be gotten through the spirit of the devil when it enters an unborn child.

In some cases, it is considered an art which can be acquired from parents and relatives. It is also considered as an infection that can be taken through food and creates a craving for human flesh and blood in a person.

It can as well be administered through incisures with sharp razor blades and medicines for becoming a witch are inserted.[127] That is why there is a lot of fear when one wakes up in the morning with what appears to be incisures on the body. It is either blood was taken from the person or foreign bodies have been inserted in the body of a person.

Use of human body parts in business by people is a common belief. Certain body parts (sexual organs – instruments of reproduction, eyes – power to see, ears – power to hear, lips and tongue – power for speech) through magic rituals are believed to have potency to attract customers in bars, shops and other businesses.

Today, even among the religious leaders there is a belief that some are approaching Prophets, Seers and Prophetess to increase the numbers of people in their congregations so as to realize more offering.

Certain witches are believed to use human labour at night to cultivate land, plant seeds, harvest crops and carry heavy loads. Because of magical use of human labour witches' harvests and yields are believed to be extraordinarily high.[128]

Today in Zambia there is still a widespread and strong belief in what is known as "ritual killings or murders", witchcraft, magic and other such happenings. This is killing of human beings for the purpose of using the victim's body parts like tongue, sexual organs, eyes, heart, for ritual purpose, especially in businesses and enhancement of personal lives. These ritual killings or murders are believed to be related to enhancement of life, wealth and businesses.

---

[126] Klaus E. Muller and Ute Ritz-Muller, Soul of Africa: Magical Rites and Traditions, 138.

[127] Joseph M., Hopkins, "Theological Students and witchcraft beliefs", *Journal of religion in Africa*, (1980), XI (1), 56 – 65.

[128] Kate Crehan, The Fractured Community: Landscapes of Power and Gender in Rural Zambia (London: University of California Press, 1997), 219-220.

Usually, people alleged to be involved are businesspeople and witches. And people do not take these killings and murders lightly. They bring agitations, resentments and animosity towards the alleged perpetrators.[129] Zambia has experienced in recent years deaths based on mob justice condemning people alleged to be ritual killers and witches.

Therefore, belief in the myths of witch-craft and Ba Kamunyama have continued and have been domesticated or accommodated in a different way within the modern life of the Zambian people, according to the times and social changes. Actually, this indicates that very little has changed in terms of cultural belief system, but only symbols that carry these beliefs have changed according to times. The meaning and interpretation of life remains the same.

A Zambian has gone to school, has travelled wide and far, has embraced modern technology to ease life and life in many ways has become easy, but when it comes to belief system and fundamental life values, still remains the same Zambian who approaches life in the same way.

This is the working and the influence of the "Zambian worldview". The root and stem of all these are the same. It is the worldview, only the off-shoots change with time. Some scholars have pointed out that nearly everywhere in Africa there is a close connection between the new materiality of wealth and witchcraft. Witchcraft in this case is intertwined with modernity.[130]

In the context of the above realities an African life in a vulnerable world through relationships. There is somehow a need for security, protection and fending off of evil of people with malicious intention to harm others through mystical means.

This has popularized prophets, seers, pastors and some men of God who act like traditional diviners but in a modern and acceptable way with recent times. It is interesting to see how modern Christian leaders have transformed themselves into modern traditional diviners. These same Christian religious leaders command a lot of respect and authority among people from both believers and non-believers, from within and outside. They have become "religious leaders without boundaries or borders".

---

[129] Times of Zambia, Wednesday, (March 4, 2015) No. 17,111.
[130] Cyprian Fisiy and Peter Geschiere, "Witchcraft, Violence and Identity: different trajectories in Postcolonial Cameroon", in *Postcolonial Identities in Africa Richard*, ed. Werbner and Terence Ranger (New Jersey: Zed Books, 1996), 194.

Chapter 3

Reality and Existence of Evil in African Traditional Religions

Understanding of evil as a concept is in some cases something relative in its interpretation. It differs from one society to another. What may be considered evil and unacceptable in one society may be differently approached in another.

With understanding of universal human rights today, the global community has to consider as evil and unacceptable certain acts. It has to be appreciated though, that in spite of some universal unacceptability of some actions taken by human beings, arguments still abound on many issues, for example, abortion, homosexuality, among others.

Understanding and origin of evil in many African traditional religions has its origin in mythology. Africa has a number of mythological and folkloristic accounts about the origin of evil. However, this is not the subject matter of our discussion. The fact still remains that the concept of evil exists in African worldview. Existence of evil is not doubted in African traditional religions. Evil is real in the life of an African.

An African experiences suffering, misfortune in form of accidents, poor harvest, barrenness, unemployment, impotency, sickness, and even death. All these can be caused by several spiritual existents. In some cases, pain and suffering are all and almost always given a religious interpretation. Misfortunes, suffering and pain are usually interpreted as due to broken relationship among people, with the world, ancestors or with God.

There is always some deeper cause for every suffering and misfortune. The religious African background always puts a link to everything and events. In this case, therefore, suffering and evil have a religious meaning because of the understanding of vital force in the context of African world-view.

This link enables the living, among the Africans, to assume what Nkemnkia calls a double existence – man is both material and a spiritual being at the same time. What happens to an African person, therefore, has a spiritual dimension to it. This is part of African spirituality and experience.

Some African are capable of transforming into a purely spiritual being and coming back into a material being again. With this capacity man is capable of doing evil (witchcraft) and at the same time doing good for society (witch doctors) and for individuals – can attack and protect, preserve and destroy, heal and cause illness.[131]

A diviner and witch doctor are a contradiction in the community. Illness for many Zambians is not just a mere physical process happening in the body of a human person, but it is something coming from some spiritual disturbance in the relationship between persons and their life world.

In this case the origin of some human suffering and evil are found both in the spiritual and material worlds. Even the sources of human prosperity originate from the same spiritual source. This makes rituals and prayers to occupy an important place in the life of African people. Rituals are means by which an African is able to understand the linkage between the material and the spiritual dimensions. The churches in Zambia are seen as instruments of this linkage between the surrounding physical world and the spiritual world.

However, it has to be pointed out that the mushrooming or proliferation of churches in the Zambian urban areas may be in some cases based on the traumas of social-cultural breakdown, psychopathological crisis, unemployment, marital problems, disease and other misfortunes that are off-shoots of complex urban life. Not only that, proliferation of churches is also good for political manipulation and power.

The more disjointed religious voices you have, the more it is good for political corruption and expediency. Segmented voice is recipe for manipulation and control. Partly this is a case for Zambia through the Ministry of Religious Affairs. Through this ministry the political

---

[131] Martin Nkafu Nkemnkia, African Vitality: A Step forward in African Thinking, 116. This gives rise to the belief, in Satanism, Witchcraft, Ritual killings etc. Some African religious leaders have the capacity to tap into this supernatural power – Vital force for healing, protection of their members from evil. This makes it a possibility for them to use the same powers for manipulation and abusing of people. A witch-finder and a religious leader can stand as a contradictory figure – revered and feared at the same time. This gives them authority and this authority can be violated, abused and used for manipulation of individuals and society.

establishment is capable of taping into religion for political support. Politicians ride on religious segmentation to manipulate the people.

Religious spaces are not only for the expression of religious beliefs but they are also political spaces for politicians. From this point of view, I would argue that religion is a symbolic power for socio-cultural and psycho-political games. At the same time, the joining of these churches may serve many people as an escape to acquire new lifestyles and shading off a state of illness, misfortune and emptiness to enter a new world of positive change and social stability.

Through religious spaces some people are able to deal with their social, political, economic and psychological vulnerability caused by believed evil. Sources of evil in African traditional religions are from both spiritual and material worlds. Both worlds play a role in daily life of people, their well-being, stability, success, and prosperity.

3.1. God as the Cause of Evil

While many Africans believe in the existence of the Supreme-being called by different names, in many instances God is perceived to be remote. However, there is a belief that he can still punish offenders in different ways for their evil committed against others. He is a God who is concerned about morality of people and their welfare. God is not aloof or indifferent to human life and how they live with one another. God is believed in African traditional religions to reward the virtuous and punish the evil doers.

Evil finds expression in many different ways that may include, killing a fellow human being, stealing, adultery, disrespect for elders, telling lies, incest, cruelty to or doing harm to other people in many different ways.[132]

Even among Zambians there is a belief that God can punish people on their offences, *"Lesa ni malyotola, ala lyotola"*. This expression is used to imply God's just punishment on an offending and transgressing person.

There are also instances where there is acceptance of misfortunes as God's way and not seen as punishments. There are certain deaths for example, that are considered to be designed by God, *"imfwa ya kwa Lesa"*, especially of very elderly people. Therefore, he is a God

---

[132] Enegho M. A. Izibili, "African Traditional Approach to the problems of evil in the world", *Stud Tribes Tribals*, 7 (1), 2009, 11 – 15.

who can punish for offenders and at the same time whose will is accepted and respected as just and normal without any tone of punishment.

At the same time God is considered as a source of human blessings. God can bless a human being with prosperity, good harvest, children, long life, good health and other blessings. Usually, God is a source of blessings for those who follow his dictates by being good, faithful, honesty, and trustworthy to others.

In God there is this contradiction, a God who can curse the evil doer and at the same time one who can bless a good person. In other African traditional religions while they have a concept of existence of God, he is however not concerned with daily life of the people.

He is a God who is considered to be faraway, *"Deus otiosus"* or *"Deus absconditus"* from the people and he only operates through the intermediaries like the ancestors. This makes the spiritual presence of God to appear absent in the performance of rituals and daily practices of religion.

Christianity came to conclude that in African traditional religions there is no belief in the supreme –being because of this indirect invocation of God. Among such traditions one may not find anything representing God, like shrines or sacrifices directly to God. On the Kasena and Dagaba people of Northern Ghana, Der had this to say:

> In account of African traditional religions, anthropologists have tended to stress the view that Africans do not sacrifice directly to God but to their ancestors. In sacrifices, whether communal or personal, it is the ancestors who are invoked, and who are called upon to accept the sacrificial offerings. God plays little or no role at all in the communal cults of these religions. Prayers are rarely addressed to him independently and although he is thought to stand behind the ancestors at ritual or religious occasions he is not directly or immediately concerned in sacrifices.[133]

While many may agree with Der about the remoteness of God from the people in African traditional religions, this is not the case for all African traditional religions. The remoteness of God may be interpreted as a description of God's transcendence, greatness and

---

[133] B.G. Der, "God and Sacrifice in the Traditional Religions of the Kasena and Dagaba of Northern Ghana", *Journal of Religion in Africa*, 11, (1980), 172 – 187.

immanence and not the real absence. It is therefore, an interpretation of the symbolic distance between human beings and God.

He is a God who is symbolically distant in his being from the human being but actively involved in human daily life. It is like the presence of a chief among his people. Sociologically a chief or a king is not generally approached by his people directly but through elders. A chief in this case is a distant figure from his people in a symbolic way.

Therefore, he cannot be approached directly by his people. God being an Elder of elders, a symbolic distance is created. In some cases, just as the King or a chief is among his people so is God considered to be actively close to the people and playing a role in their daily lives.[134] God continues to bring human beings into being with the co-operation of human beings through human sexual intercourse. God through human sexual relationship, he works with his people.

For example, among the Nyakyusa people of East Africa God is very present and works with his people closely in many different ways like conception, creation of twins, giving strength to work, among others. In this case every event like procreation of human beings has a metaphysical orientation and explanation, God is present.[135] Therefore, God being involved in the life of the people indirectly is capable of punishing the evil doers or through the intermediary, the ancestors.

In this case, the prayers and offering made to the intermediaries are ultimately offered to God through them. Intermediaries are considered as agents through whom God operates and bestows his blessings on people.

Moral order in this case is defended and protected by the ancestors but only because it has been established by God. Ancestors therefore, can punish on behalf of God for not respecting the moral order laid down by God. This is not evil but considered as a just punishment from God. God can punish people and society through,

---

[134] Bolaji E. Idow, Olodumare: God in Yoruba Belief, (London: A & B Book Dist Inc, 1994), 140 – 147. The Chief that becomes too common among the people slowly loses the mystical being and authority. In Zambia chiefs lost their mystical authority by bringing them into the public through politics. The symbolic power of chiefs has been eroded because they have become so common.

[135] Monica. Wilson, Communal Rituals of the Nyakyusa, (London: Routledge, 1959), 156.

for example, disease, floods, droughts etc. Punishment and blessing can happen at a personal and society levels.

3.2. Spirits of the Living-Dead as the Cause of Evil

In the Zambian context there are instances where it is believed that the spirits of the dead can send misfortune to the living as a form of punishment. These spirits can cause bad luck (ishamo).

It is believed these spirits can be washed on others to cause psychoneurotic symptoms and havoc in families, marriages and during sleep.[136] This makes dreams and their interpretation very important. Dreams are a source of communication among the living and sometimes with the dead. The living dead sometimes communicate with the living through dreams.

Seers, diviners and some ritual religious leaders are able to see what is happening in the life of people through dreams. These ritual leaders are able to communicate with the living dead and pass on the message to the relatives about what has happened in their families.

Sometimes misfortune in this case is interpreted as a consequence of intervention of ancestral spirits to punish their descendants because they have violated certain important rules for the order of society, family order and life. For example, one may be punished for having sexual intercourse with very close blood relatives, father and daughter, brother and sister or son and mother or having sexual intercourse with a Widow or widower who has not yet been traditionally cleansed. It is even worse if such an act leads to pregnancy.

Killing a person is another instance in which the spirit of the dead is believed to come back to haunt someone who caused the death. This brings disorder and confusion in the kinship of the family which affects even the dead. It becomes a taboo.

Spirits of the dead can punish one for a taboo committed. Actually, here they do not speak of evil but punishment from the

---

[136] Clive, Dillon-Malone, *Journal of Religion in Africa*, Vol. XVII, 1 (1987), 2-31. There is a strong belief that if you had caused some suffering or misfortune to someone who later died, the spirit of the person might come back to haunt you as a punishment. There are instances where the dead are seen in visions by the perpetrators of their deaths. In severe situations these visions can cause depressions and derangements.

spirits of the dead.[137] Sickness is generally perceived as punishment from the spirits of the ancestors. One can become a victim because of non-observance of social norms of society. There is a strong belief among Africans that ancestors are capable of withdrawing their protection from a socially ailing and transgressive person.

The transgressor begins to experience misfortunes and hardships in general, bad luck and life to some extent loses meaning.[138] The sufferings caused by the ancestors are usually considered to be temporary punishments which are aimed at making a victim to pay attention to some wrongful acts committed. These are punishments that are meant for correction, remorsefulness and repentance.[139]

In certain circumstances the spirits of the dead are believed to block prosperity, human fertility, they can make a person or culprits deranged or go mad and they can be the causes of certain unexplained illnesses that cannot be addressed by modern medical services. One becomes afflicted with spirits because of failure to observe social obligations and norms.[140]

Today healing of family trees is proving to be popular and centre of spiritual and psychological attention. This is healing of families from the past misdeeds committed by the dead and living relatives which have caused different blockades and bondages in the lives of the living members.[141]

According to Nyangisa, certain families experience different illnesses and misfortunes that can be traced back to their dead relatives or ancestors. These may include among many others unexplained missing of relatives, divorces, similar deaths, suicides, lack of proper and stable marriages, fornication and adultery and other misfortunes.

In many African cultural settings, the dead become more powerful spiritually than when they were physically alive. In some instances, their misdeeds do not go to the grave with them. They continue to haunt the living through their family trees. African traditional

---

[137] Valeer Neckebrouck, "The Nature of African Traditional Religion", (Leuven: lecture, University of Leuven, 2000)

[138] Bernard B. M. Lubumbe, Sunday Eucharistic Celebration: A critical overview (Ndola: Mission Press, 2011), 40.

[139] Benjamin, C. Ray, African Religions: Symbol, Ritual and Community (New Jersey: Prentice Hall, 2000), 106.

[140] Clive, Dillon-Malone, *Journal of Religion in Africa*, 2 – 31.

[141] John Ooko, Nyangisa, Healing your Family Tree (Limuru – Kenya: Franciscan Kolbe Press, 2010), 20 – 23.

religions have a remedy to such misfortunes through traditional rituals, like rituals of cleansing and putting to rest the spirits of the dead.[142]

3.3. The Living as the Cause of Evil

Moral life in African traditions is emphasized on the basis of the good character of a person. A good character of a person includes, kindness, generosity, hospitality, justice, respect for elders and others. Opposite of these become a source of evil for many African people.

Therefore, evil at another level is located in the human world, in human character and actions. In this case human beings are the source of evil. The evil has its source in the heart of human persons because of jealousy, hatred and uncontrolled ambitions. It is this jealousy and uncontrolled ambitions that can lead one into the practice of witchcraft and Satanism.[143]

Witches are the sources of evil out of jealousy, self-enhancement and uncontrolled ambitions through the use of *ubwanga*– magical charms or through manipulation of spirits for the wicked purposes.[144] This is one of the serious and highest violations of moral order in African traditional society. It is the employment of mystical forces to harm one's neighbour and one's kin.

Mystical forces in this case can be used either for good or bad intentions. This is a popular belief among Zambians that there are within the community some people who are bent on harming others through illness, death and bad luck. The attitude towards such malicious activities is to deal with these issues from a metaphysical point of view.

Today these can be dealt with by diviner, prophet, priest, pastor, man of God and a healer. Satanism falls in this category as a cause for evil. Witches and Satanists incarnate the evil forces that disrupt the harmonious life of society. They are anti-social and anti-human elements or beings. Both can attack and even kill people including relatives.

They make use of substances and objects believed to be imbued with supernatural powers. They are believed to use spells on others. All elements of this type cause evil by perversion of the sacred.

---

[142] Ibid. 20 – 22.
[143] Benjamin, C. Ray, African Religions: Symbol, Ritual and Community, 106.
[144] Ibid., 2 – 31.

Therefore, they cannot be dealt with scientific means but spiritual and religious approaches.

This points to the importance of rituals in African traditional religions. Rituals help to preserve and protect the community from spiritual harm and misfortunes.

Therefore, an African cannot do without religious rituals. They are an important aspect of African life that cannot be dismissed easily. Rituals are therefore, part of the African world-view. Rituals connect the two important worlds of an African, the material and the spiritual. African society without meaningful rituals can become transgressive, aggressive, violent and spiritually broken. Rituals hold the African worlds together, stable and in balance.

Chapter 4

Ritual-Power in African Traditional Religions

Leaderships in many African cultural settings have symbolic meanings. Just as the world of an African is interconnected in its elements, so is leadership in African context. Leadership is also connected to all the elements that make up the African cosmology. Leadership impacts very much on the African world.

An African traditional leader is a priest, king/chief, economist, politician, religious and everything that gives meaning to the life in the world. A traditional leader cannot be separated from any of the realms of an African world. A traditional leader belongs both to the material and metaphysical worlds.

Life of a traditional leader oscillates between these two worlds. Therefore, this separation of politicians, economists, chiefs/ kings and religious leaders is something new in the context of many African societies. It is a western approach to African life-world.

A traditional African leader carries all the fundamental aspects of the cosmology on his body and his articulation with the outer world. The way of life of any leadership in the African context is based on the articulation in all the spheres of life. A leader in African context is a politician, an economist, a chief or a king and a religious figure.

African traditional leaders are endowed with both sacred and secular duties without separating them in any way. Some have a sacred duty of making rain, causing rich harvest and upholding the traditional cosmic order in harmony. In fact, their bodies are a representation of their world and society. They are an intermediate between the physical and spiritual worlds. As religious leaders they are usually considered as ritual specialists who mediate between the two worlds.[145] An African traditional leader is as well a person of rituals.

A traditional leader has authority in every area of life, political, religious, economic and social. A traditional leader still remains a symbolic figure of cosmic order and stability. That is why traditional leaders are called "fathers" of their people.

---

[145] Stephen, Ellis and Gerrie ter Haar, *The Journal of Modern African Studies*, Vol. 36, No. 2 (June, 1998), 175-201.

For these leaders to hold the world together, they possess supernatural powers that can give guarantee for growth in prosperity, harvest and victories over enemies.[146] They have the ability to bring different worlds together. They can act as mediators between the "living dead" and the "living", the supernatural and the natural worlds.

The term supernatural in this discourse is used contextually. The term in this context is being used as an emic concept. Meaning it has to be defined within its meaningfulness of a particular context not as a concept of science. From an emic point of view, the concept has diverse meanings as there are cultures.

Here it is being used as a reality that transcends the natural empirical reality. In this case it includes the extraordinary, the mysterious, such as magic, sorcery, curses and practices that hold meaning for all different cultures.[147]

It is a term that describes phenomena that is beyond the "normal" human perception and experience. It includes religious, magical, spiritual, metaphysical, occult and para-psychological aspects of cultures. African life is both a participation in the supernatural and material worlds in this sense.[148] Religious leaders in African context are believed to have authority over all these aspects.

However, life is mediated by a figure above the recipient who may include chiefs, kings and household leadership. These are not only regarded as personages with power of administration. They are spiritually connected by a mystical, religious bond with the outer-world. Leadership therefore, at every level has a function of transmitting life which encompasses the whole human life.[149] This can be clearly seen in the way some political leadership play out their role in Africa.

Many African political (civic) leaders carry some religious undertones as well. President Fredrick Chiluba could be cited as such an example. He acted as a politician and a religious leader.

---

[146] Klaus E. Muller and Ute Ritz-Muller, Soul of Africa: Magical Rites and Traditions, 380.

[147] Lehman Arthur and James Myers, ed. "The Anthropological Study of religion", in *Magic, Witchcraft and Religion: An Anthropological Study of Supernatural*, 2nd ed. (Mountain View, CA, Mayfield Publishing Company, 1989), 3.

[148] Stephen D. Glazier, ed. Anthropology of Religion (London: Praeger Publishers, 1999), 110 - 111.

[149] Benezet Bujo, African Theology: In its Social Context, 19-20.

He would influence the populous in both areas. From an African point view this is not strange because an African leader is both religious and political entity among the people. Leadership in many African settings is a symbolic leadership. It is a leadership with many different meanings. In many African contexts you never find a leader who is purely political or purely religious but may have an expression of both.

In Zambia the question still looms as to whether Alice Lenshina Mulenga with her Lumpa church was a political or religious leader. Depending on different symbolic approaches, some may look at her as a political leader and some as a religious leader. However, she embraced both worlds, natural and supernatural worlds (a prophetess of God who had an experience with Jesus Christ), political (interpreted as a symbol of resistance to foreign domination) and religious worlds (anti-witchcraft campaigner, sexual cleansing, and a mystic).

It is well known that Lumpa Church became a tool for cultural, religious and political emancipation which saw the missionaries and colonialists as suppressors of African culture, political and religious emancipation.[150] Trying to separate these two is not easy because they are intertwined by the thread of African cosmology.

Lenshina is a very good example of a symbolic leadership on whose body two worlds played out without separation and distinction. Political players in Africa therefore, do not just use religion to increase their political popularity but also to have access to the spiritual world as a resource in the constant struggle in securing advantage over political opponents.[151] This belief in this spiritual resource and its influence on politics sends alarming bells to politicians when a religious leaders starts to win popularity among masses. The case of the defrocked former archbishop of Lusaka in Zambia, Emmanuel Milingo is a good example.[152]

Leadership therefore, is seen and considered as an embodiment of success, wealth, power and control. More often than not leaders

---

[150] Alice Lenshina Mulenga Myth Unveiled, WWW.zedcorner.com/the- life-of- alice -lenshina-mulenga-lenshina myth-unveiled/. Accessed on 14.04.2019.

[151] Stephen Ellis and Gerrie ter Haar, "Politics and African Religious Traditions", *The Journal of Modern African Studies*, Vol. 36, No. 2, June (1998), 175-201.

[152] Hugo, Hinfelaar, "Bemba-speaking Women of Zambia in a country of Religious Change (1832-1992)", *Journal of Religion in Africa*, Vol. 26, No. 2 (1994), 216 – 219.

especially in Africa and Zambia in particular articulate themselves as fulcrums or centres of their societies and communities.

Other leaderships have to be identified with the centre for their success. In most cases the same leadership is not accountable to anyone or institution but to the divine being. This gives leadership whether civil or religious more power to manipulate their followers and clients. People sometimes invest their lives in them for anything and cannot be questioned.

People become so dependent on them and feel powerless without them. The leaders become their lifeline for the supply of divine and material successes just like the traditional chiefs. Divine interventions can only come to people through them because these are able to tap into the spiritual world. This can be the justification of the irrationality and rationality of the religious experiences in Zambia.

The above exposition has an indication that religious leadership in the context of Africa has a symbolic bias. Religious leaders are divine figures who are able to tap into the Divine and others not. This puts religious leaders at higher plane and pedestal than the rest and it is this that gives them authority, power and control sometimes that cannot be questioned.

In contemporary religious sociological studies this is referred to as "religious exceptionalism" and laws of nature, culture, morality do not apply.[153] This goes across most religious groupings, especially in Zambia. In some instances, because of the authority which is taken for granted religious leaders have misappropriated institutional resources, abused church members in untold ways and gotten away with it.

Religious leaders are often not questioned on many issues. Their authority is divine. There is strong belief for example among traditional Catholics and other religious groupings that it is a taboo to speak ill about a priest or a man of God, not even his sins to another person.

By doing this you bring a curse on yourself. Questioning their authority is questioning the divine, God's authority and their power of connecting the obvious. Could this be the source of the irrationality that we are seeing and experiencing today regarding religious experiences?

---

[153] Theconversation.com, Why South Africans are prone to falling for charlatans in church. Accessed on 21.03.2021.

4.1. Power and Authority of Ritual Leaders

Every African society has ritual leaders who have the power and authority to help communicate between humanity and the spiritual realm. This communication is done through rituals. These religious leaders today can play the role of traditional diviners, prophets and pastors.

Today many titles have been devised for religious leaders or the ritual specialists, like men of God, apostles, bishops, evangelists and many other titles. Their social and religious roles range from, preaching the word of God, healing, interpretation of dreams, tackling emotional and psychological disorders, infertility, social misfortunes, Satanismto dealing in some cases with medical conditions and economic challenges of the people.

This should not be seen just as a simple old form of traditionalism because of the desperate and hopeless situation of the people. The point is that there is great awareness of existing spiritual powers and forces in the cosmology that play a role in the daily life of people. Need for spiritual mediums to tap into the spiritual powers and forces for the good of individuals and communities is part of life.[154]

4.2. Ritual Leaders as Intermediaries

It cannot be argued that Zambia is experiencing the proliferation of spiritual figures who are working under the influence of spirits in the name of God. Here it has to be pointed out that this is not a new phenomenon. It is something that has been in existence for a long time taking a different way of expression at particular time in religious history of the people. Zambia culturally has believed in spirit possession from olden times though not in uniformity and homogeneously (under the name of Jesus) but in plurality under different spirits. This is true for Africa in general and in particular cultural settings. Today what is emphasized is the possession by the spirit of God in the name Jesus Christ.

Therefore, spirit possession is nothing new. It is only a question of which spirit has possessed someone. The other new aspect to spirit

---

[154] Lesley A. Sharp, "The Power of Possession in Northwest Madagascar – Contesting Colonial and National Hegemonies", *Spirit Possession: Modernity and Power in Africa*, Ed. Heike Behrend and Ute Luig (Kampala: Fountain Publishers, 1999), 13.

possession is that the go-between, intermediary figures[155] (mediumistic figures) have become part of global and trans-cultural phenomenon. People from Zambia can go as far as Nigeria in West Africa, Tanzania, Kenya, and South Africa for prayers and healing. Meaning that spirit possession is no longer confined to the local community and language.

The religious leaders as the go-between act as intermediaries between the two different worlds, the physical and the spiritual worlds. By the fact that they are under the influence of the spirit of God they are able to connect the two worlds for the good of the community and individuals.

4.3 Mediumistic Role of Ritual Leaders

Generally, many African traditional religions hold it that there is One Creator (Mulungu, Lesa, "Mulenga" – the great Artist, "Chansa" – the One who spreads out, "Chanda" – the One who covers out) the creator of a dynamic universe. However, to many Africans this God is remote from the daily human experiences of people.

He can be approached through media such as ritual specialists, ancestors, prophets and religious leaders. These are persons who have the ability to make contact with the other world.

As Soltyk points out, mediumistic role can manifest itself in various ways. This may include changes in someone's mental and physical state like ecstasy, elation, possession and embodiment of spirits. Medium have the capacity to penetrate thoughts, seeing reality from a distance, clairvoyance, sensing spiritual traces left by unseen human psyche, sensing phenomena concerning future or past things, bilocation and causing distant occurrences.[156] This theory can explain the reification of the position of religious leaders in Zambia. These are considered people with special powers that make them enter the

---

[155] This discourse uses the term "go-between" to include all spiritual, religious figures that have come out on the scene in recent times, like prophets, pastors, evangelists, apostles, elders, men of God, intercessors, healers, diviners, priests, etc. All of them in some way have authority to claim to have power to tap into the spiritual realm on behalf of clients in different needs (psychological, economical, relational, spiritual, social and medical) and to help their communities. Today the line of differentiation among these groups of people is becoming more blurred and diminishing slowly. One religious leader may perform more than one of the roles of the listed figures.

[156] Malgorzata, Soltyk, "Invoking Spirits", *Love One Another*, No. 47.

realm of transcendent. They are under the influence of the spirit of God, the Holy Spirit.

Many Christian churches today have integrated well the aspect of spirit possession in many ways using the symbolisms of the Bible, cross, holy water, holy and anointing oils, and speaking in tongues etc., coupled with charismatic orientation of the leaders.

Popularity of religious leadership, like in old cultic times, is based on the efficacy, reality or perceived and on the leader's counsel, psychic support and in helping people realize their desires and needs.

Today the prestige of the religious leaders is seen in the context of intermediary. Prestige indicates the success of a religious leader in this role. What is important is the fact that they are able to control and dispense mystical powers that can restore certainty, harmony and balance in human and cosmic realms.

New and modern religious leaders like the traditional ritual leaders are considered mediators of power between God and their followers through rituals. Some have considered this experience as a usurpation of authority of traditional witchdoctors, Diviners, Sangomas and traditional healers.[157] This we can argue is more than just usurpation of traditional religious power, but a religious tapping into the African belief system.

Coupled with the above-mentioned authority, it has to be mentioned that human beings have the capacity to suspend their individuality to become part of the larger group.

This happens in religions through ritual experiences in mass healing events, charismatic gatherings and rallies, demonstrations, riots etc. The individual enters something greater and beyond the self which over-shadows individuality. This may explain some of the spiritual phenomena of "irrationality" in today's religion.

A religious leader being a representation of the beyond, represents something greater than the individual. The individual loses the capacity of individuality and enters into the greater authority of the religious leader – representing the spiritual world. Therefore, the "irrationality" being experienced today in some churches can be explained through this theory of human's capacity to lose individuality to become part of the larger experience, unquestionable

---

[157] Jamaica Gleaner, Church Mafia the greatest Threat to Africa's Progress, Jamaica – gleaner.com, Religion and culture/church mafia the biggest threat to Africa's progress. Accessed on 02/09/2019.

authority and power through a ritual. In some way there is loss of the self into spiritual experience or the spirit.

4.4. Nature and Importance of African Ritual

Rituals are very important in an African setting because of their expressive and instrumental role in harmonizing the world-view and the interconnectedness of different realms of life of an African. That is, between the visible and the invisible worlds. A ritual serves as weaving some threads of life. A ritual ties and connects life to the source.

A ritual in essence therefore, is more expressive than informative. It is more mystical than rational. A ritual in this case can be considered as an instrument of power in itself and the ritual leader. A ritual is an institutionalized symbolic rite which is believed to bring about some desired or preventing some undesired end to happen.[158] A ritual has the power to tap into the mystical energy for the betterment of individuals and community.

As a symbol a ritual can refer to objects, ideas, belief or some pattern of behaviour which represent some underlying rationale to which a cultural value is attached. This makes a ritual meaningful to some and not to others because of its symbolism.

A ritual is performed within the context of the belief system and world-view of the people. To some a ritual may appear only as empty ceremonial action or social performance and entertainment.[159]

On this Talcott and Holiss argue further to say that ritual actions cannot just be considered irrational or pseudo-irrational on the basis of pre-scientific erroneous knowledge, but should be considered of being different character and not to be measured by the standards intrinsic rationality. A ritual in this case cannot be considered irrelevant on the basis that it is irrational to ones way of thinking.[160]

Rituals are performed at different stages and seasons in African traditional life and the life of the world in terms of seasons. They can

---

[158] John Beattie, Other Cultures: Aims, Methods and Achievements in Social Anthropology (London: Routledge, 1964), 202.

[159] John Beatie, "On understanding Ritual", *Rationality*, ed. Bryan Wilson (Oxford: Basil Blackwell, 1977), 242.

[160] Talcott Parsons, "The Structure of Social Action" (Glencoe: The free Press, 1949), 431; Martin Hollis, "Reason and Ritual", *Rationality*, ed. Bryan Wilson (Oxford: Basil Blackwell, 1977), 233.

take place at birth, name –giving, fishing, hunting, puberty, wedding, healing, funeral and memorials for the dead. They can as well be performed at different seasons, cultivation of the land, planting, harvesting and before and after every season.

There are as well rituals of affliction, crisis, installation, stability of life, cleansing and rituals performed before and after love making between husband and wife. In some of these celebrations and moments, members of the family and larger community are vitally expected to participate to experience together the transformative power of the ritual and reconnecting members to one another. Some are public and others are private rituals, like in the case of bedroom, some puberty and initiation rituals.

All these activities have some bearing on African spirituality. African rituals are an expression of African belief, religious life and spirituality. They are an expression of African life, hope and expectations.

Rituals being symbolic give support to human life through which the supernatural and spiritual mediators hold the community together in many different ways. Rituals have an orientation of social and spiritual integration. They have inherent capacity to bring the community together politically, socially and culturally in a spiritual sense.

A ritual has the power to strengthen the bonds with the transcendent though Emile Durkheim contends that the sense of transcendent is the community itself. God remains the existence of the community and nothing more. God does not exist but the community.

God is a projection of the existence of the community. "God is the community'. Here it does not mean that God works through the community, but that God does not exist, only the community does. God in this case exists as a sociological projection.

According to Durkheim, it is the community acting through the rituals to bring about cohesion and what the community desires. What the community desires is expressed through the ritual. Through this argument, Durkheim rejects the spiritual aspect of the ritual. The ritual remains just at the level of a sociological fact without any religious dimension.[161]

---

[161] Emile Durkheim, Elementary Forms of the Religious Life (London: Hollen Press, 1915), 226.

The instruments in a ritual therefore, are symbolic. That is why a ritual is not univocal and conservative. A ritual speaks different languages with different voices about different things, times and events of life to different people.

Rituals being multi-vocal can include conflicted social, cultural, political and economic realities. Rituals have power to objectify different social conflicts of everyday life in helping people to transcend them. Rituals have the power of mystification of events and experiences.

That is, power of the transcendental over the everyday experiences and events. They dramatize the process through which the vitality of everyday life and experiences is conquered by the transcendence. A ritual in this case has the power to control events and circumstances and projecting this power and control into the future.[162]

Therefore, rituals speak a language of the people in the "now" and not just in the past and the future. Rituals respond to the life of the people as it is lived in the present. When a ritual is fulfilled in the present, it gives hope for the future. In this case, the future is worked out in the present.[163]

Religious beliefs played out in rituals are responsible for changes that take place at the heart of life of individuals and society in the now and the future. Rituals strengthen good relationships with the supernatural, fellow human beings and the environment. This makes a person going through the ritual feel protected against all forces that are life threatening.[164]

Rituals are therefore a question of life and survival for society and individuals. Rituals are instruments of healing individual bodies (corporeal bodies) and society as a body (social bodies). This is where the importance of ritual lies. Where there are no rituals, physical and social aggression, violence of every kind, psychological imbalances, loss of personhood and sense of personal boundaries and abuses abounds.

---

[162] Maurice Bloch, Ritual, History and Power: Selected papers in Social Anthropology (London: The Athlone Press, 1989).

[163] Jean Comaroff, Body of Power Spirit of Resistance (Chicago: The University of Chicago Press, 1985), 119.

[164] Laurent, Mpongo, "Contemporary African celebration of the blessing of the Baptismal water in Roman Rite", *Concilium*, (1985), 62 – 68.

A society without rituals is likely to easily descend into violence and disintegration of human bodies and the society. Rituals heal human bodies and the body of society. Rituals bind society as whole and integrates the human individual bodies into whole bodies.

That is why the replacement of the traditional rituals by the foreign ones has not only contributed to the disintegration of the society but at some deeper level it has led to disintegrated human bodies which are vulnerable to the outside world. Rituals are for the good of both human bodies and society body.

Songs, dances and prayers are some of the formal features that characterize ritual performance. Through rituals religion stimulates strong emotions through the techniques of physical ordeals, crowding, noise, rhythm, exhaustion, starvation, gratification, shock, among others. These are the characteristics of today's healing and prosperity churches. These rituals are unquestionable and the ritual leader as a leader stimulates the responses from the participants.

This situation creates unequal relationships between the performer and the participant, leader and the follower, supcrordinate and the subordinate. This builds up an automatic dominance in the ritual relationship.[165]

This is the point at which we see sometimes the "irrationality" of what we see and hear about what is happening in some of the proliferating churches of prophets and some pastors in Zambia and across Africa. At this point even manipulation and abuse of any kind is accommodated due to the imbalance in expression of mystical and ritual power.

How do you explain a situation where a pastor directs his congregation to remove their underwear, wave them in the air during a church service for healing purposes, to attract angels from heaven and people do it out of the trust they have for their ritual leader?[166] A pastor performs miracles on female congregants by kissing them – "kissing anointing" to transmit the power of God to people and a way of delivering people.[167] Or pastor anointing and blessing of brooms and giving them to the members of the church to use to

---

[165] Sandra T Barnes, "Ritual, Power and outside knowledge", *Journal of religion in Africa*, (1990), XX (3), 248-268.

[166] www.standardmedia.co.ke, pastor orders congregation to remove underwear, wave it in the air. Accessed on, 01.02.2021.

[167] www.tuko.co.ke, Pastor performs miracles on female congregants by kissing.

sweep evil and demons from their homes, offices and shops and the same pastor alleging having visited heaven during which he took pictures with his Samsung Galaxy phone.[168] In another religious context, a pastor rubbing olive oil on the vagina of his church members as a way of casting out evil spirits.[169] All these spiritual experiences can be explained from the above taken for granted dominance and control by the religious and ritual leaders.

Ritual leaders exert ritual authority on their clients. This leadership and their ritual actions are unquestionable and undoubtable. This attitude finds its origin in the expression of traditional rituals by diviners, witch finders, prophets, medicine men and women whose expression of power over participants is not questionable or challenged for fear of challenging divine powers.

Rituals in this case restrict debate, critical thinking and contestation. Traditional ritual leaders like diviners and witch finders, including Christian ritual leaders have in some circumstances requested very expensive material things from their clients like, money, bicycles, cars, shoes, suits, blankets, expensive plates, chickens, among others.

Today in cash economies, the most requested for gift is money or cash in form of tithes. This is the domestication of modernity through cultural spiritual logic. At the same time, rituals mean different things to different people at different times and circumstances because they are symbolic in nature in relation to the participants.

Through the symbolism of a ritual, a ritual becomes the medium through which participants define their own experiences. The ritual becomes a site for new history in the making or being created for individuals and society.[170] Places of ritual performance act as weaving rooms for connecting people to the spiritual world, one another and to the self.

This becomes part of the understanding of a religious ritual, its unquestionable aspect in its performance. It carries some aspects of subordination, social control, aggression and domination. Of course, this situation can be construed, changed and translated into abuse,

---

[168] www.tuko.co.ke

[169] Lailasnews.com

[170] John. D. Kelly, and Martha Kaplan, "History, Structure and Ritual", *Annual Review of Anthropology*, (1990) 19: 119 – 150.

aggression and irrational. What may appear irrational, I should hasten to say may have some deep rationality behind it in the participant.

A ritual is not an expression of power, but its power itself. Sometimes behind the ritual there are layers and layers of deeper meanings. Rituals have some esoteric knowledge derived from their performance. It is this knowledge which one cannot challenge or question.

That is why ritual leaders and authorities are considered among the knowledgeable figures in African communities.[171] These are sometimes referred to as "abamano", the "wise and the knowledgeable" among the Bemba people of Northern Zambia. These are personages who are able to see what ordinary people cannot see. Their eyes are very piercing and able to see into the past, present and the future.

They are able to see what others cannot see and perceive. They sniff like hunting dogs and hunters who able to read the trail of the hunted victim. This is where their wisdom and knowledge lie. It is in connecting the known to the unknown and vice-versa. Even what can be scientifically verified can still be perceived from a spiritual point of view without seeing any contradictions between science and religion.

Among the Ndembu people, one of the celebrated aspects of a ritual symbolism is the power of the ritual to make visible, audible, and tangible beliefs, ideas, values, sentiments, and psychological dispositions that cannot be perceived in normal circumstances. Through the ritual the unknown, invisible or the hidden and what is private is made public or laid bare. This is known as "ku-solola"- "to make visible" or "to reveal".[172]

Religious leaders in many African cultures and Zambia in particular have domesticated this same traditional role of the diviner. Some ritual leaders are able to see what science cannot see.

Epilepsy, HIV, goiter, cancers, stealing, and suicides have all spiritual orientations that can be interpreted. Even the spirits of being glued to social media, genetic diseases, thwarting of careers and limitations to successful achievements, businesses, impotence, failure to conceive, alcoholism, can be delivered. All these can be

---

[171] Sandra T Barnes, "Ritual, Power and Outside Knowledge", *Journal of religion in Africa* (1990), 256-257.

[172] Victor Turner, The Forest of Symbols: Aspect of Ndembu Ritual (London: Cornell University Press, 1967), 48–49.

approached as spiritual existents. However, in many cases though these evil spirits can be identified, their sources are not mentioned and known. In traditional diagnosis sources of different evil spirits are traced and brought to the open. African traditional religions believe in the patients' exteriorization of the hidden inner illnesses through somatic complaints.

These somatic complaints take the form of stomachache, headache, backache, fear, loss of energy (depression), loss of appetite, blockades between the body and the outer-world, aggressiveness, loss of self-control (hysteria) etc.

Sometimes insistence on physical medicines and X-rays neglect the real illness and leads to over treatment and somatic fixation, that is being fixed on the body which in this case is only a language expressing some underlining challenges.

Physical complaints through the body are only an expression of the interior spiritual challenge. In some cases, a broken body, through physical illness, indicates the broken spiritual walls or boundaries and dissolving of individual selfhood. Good health means coherent, balanced separation and relation between the centre and the periphery, inside and outside. The task of the ritual leader is to re-create the boundaries of the body space and social space into limits.

However, both religious and traditional ritualists connect what is known to the unknown through certain knowledge. They have a role of making the invisible, visible, to reveal what is hidden in the life of people. This supports the idea that rituals are both expressive as well as instrumental in character.

In every ritual something is being expressed but at the same time a ritual enacts the state of affairs that is hoped for.[173] This is one of the most important aspects of a ritual among Zambians today. It is its instrumentalization fact of bringing about what is desired by the participant in the ritual. Rituals are not performed for their own sake but performed for expectant results of participants.

Today in Zambia a true pastor, prophet, priest, evangelist, elder, man of God, intercessor is one who is able to see what others cannot see and the authority on this is not questionable or contested. Today these religious leaders excel in insight, imagination and fluency in language. These are able to see why one is not progressing in life

---

[173] John Beattie, Other Cultures – Aims, Methods and Achievements in Social Anthropology, 204.

(prosperity); business does not grow, persistent of illness, family misunderstandings and curses etc. Here the question of context of the larger society is not related to the particular.

For example, general challenges of the larger society are not questionable but only the challenges of individuals. One who is not employed does not look at lack of employment in general in their societies but why one is not employed. A sick person does not question and bring into perspective other contributing factors, like falling standards of medical facilities or lack of medicines and numbers of people who are afflicted by the same disease.

What is brought into spotlight is individual broken and sick body. Today's pastors, priests and prophets are able to explain the fate of individuals and what should be done at an individual level and not at the level of society. Many religious leaders are not ready to confront the sources of poverty, illnesses and other social challenges from the point of view of society policies and governance. Instead, they invite people for prayers, fasting, healing, exorcism and giving gifts to God.

Today many churches including the traditional ones have entered this circle. Sometimes there is no clear line between Christian religious men and traditional diviners. I would hasten to argue that religious men and women of modern churches are performing the role of the traditional diviners and seers. They have become modernized traditional healers and diviners. What has changed are symbols and not the logic of practice.

A prophet in South Africa, of some religious ministry preaches with a huge snake around his neck or in his arms or on the pulpit during church services. The same prophet convinced his congregation to eat grass and drink petrol.[174] A Ghanaian prophet, Messiah Enyonyam Johns made a woman member of the congregation to strip herself naked in church in order to pray for her to get rid of barrenness.[175]

Another South African prophet ordered members of his congregation to remove their under wears and wave them in the air to attract angels from heaven while holding their private parts. In

---

[174] "Prophet uses a big snake in church", https://www.zambianobserver.com/prophet-uses-a-chi-big-snake-in-church/. Accessed on 24.07.2019.

[175] "Fake Prophet finally arrested, woman taken for questioning", https://www.zambianobserver.com/fake-prophet-finally-arrested-woman-taken-for-questioning/ . accessed on 27.08.2019.

performing this ritual, the prophet told them that the angels can impregnate women and bless men in the name of Jesus to have children.[176] Of course, the importance and centrality of the body in the consciousness of every society is critical to understand the dramaturgical of rituals. The human body is a reality of selfhood and at the same time a mode of mediation upon the world.

As Comaroff has put it, the human body is a "base" on which human values are engraved.[177] In the context of rituals human body becomes an object for engraving values of prosperity, cleansing, healing, power, good health and fertility.

Sexual abuses are accommodated through this spiritual understanding about the body. It is on the bodies of Pastors, Prophets, Men of God and Evangelists that embodiments of these values are witnessed. A desirable body is the body of the man of God and what it portrays from outside, health, riches and prosperity. In Zambia, a religious prophet is alleged to have buried a goat and cat as fetishes in his church for the purpose of deliverance of church members from poverty and satanic attacks in the name of Jesus.[178]

All these prophets are popular "men of God". From face value these appear to be very irrational ways of approaching religion. However, one is able to see how traditional beliefs have been accommodated and domesticated in the new found Christian religion.

The new religious movements are creating ontological spaces for life meaning. They are places of spiritual, cultural and social deconstructions. The main line traditional churches have left a gap in the lives of many people which is now being filled by new Christian approaches that are building on traditional logic and world-view.

There is something that is missing that people yearn for. These new churches are playing a role of pacifying and helping people to integrate themselves in the complex society of illusory modernity and capitalism.

---

[176] "Video, Prophet Mboro asking congregants to remove their under-wears and wave them", https://www.zambianoserver.com/video-prophet-mboro-askingcongrgants-to-remove-their-underwears-and-wave-them/. Accessed on 25.08.2019.

[177] Jean, Comaroff, Body of Power Spirit of Resistance, 6-7.

[178] "Ndola Pastor buries a goat and a cat in his church",
http://www.zambianobserver.com/ndola-pastor-buries-a-goat-anda-cat-in-his-church/. Accessed on 25.08.2019.

These new churches re-channel people's discontentment, loneliness and despair in the face of hardships into a community were divine energy binds them together to share hopes and failures. Whether the healing and prosperity churches are effective or not, for people, this is not important. What counts is the space where individuals are able to reconcile with their past, social illusions, disappointing modernity, challenges and life betrayals.

The ritual spaces of these new religious movements act as spaces of bringing out, shading off and deconstructing the inner conflicts and social conflicts within individual human bodies and among human interactions. Therefore, Zambia's social crisis is not only economic but a crisis of life meaning.

There is a yearning for understanding experiences and to give significance to life in the complex society. Many people are struggling to make sense of their experiences in the fast-changing society.[179]

This interpretation of inner and social conflicts is close to Karl Marx theory of social conflict leading to social change (conflictual relationship between infrastructure and superstructure). Rapid capitalistic changes (infrastructure) have effects on the religion (superstructure).

The infrastructure puts the superstructure into some imbalance leading to subjective experiences of alienation. However, Marx does not interpret his theory to include the individual human inner conflict. It only talks about social conflicts between groups, in this case the conflict between infrastructure and the superstructure.

It can be argued further using this conflict theory that even at personal and individual level this conflict takes place. This can take the form of a spiritual dimension. This is a conflict between social and external conditions and the inner selves of individuals. It is conflict between the inner spiritual self and the social conditions.

According to Marx economic conditions determine the world of ideas of the people including religious beliefs. Some of these ideas can be very conflictual to the establishment and social status quo. With the enforcement of the law and norms by modern society the expression of conflict is curtailed.

Social norms and laws push further the conflict into the spiritual space. Instead, people have to find other means in which inner (being

---

[179] James Ferguson, Expectations of Modernity: Myths and Meanings of Urban life on the Zambian Copperbelt (Los Angeles: University of California Press, 1999), 14.

uprooted from socio-economic, cultural and traditional meaningfulness) social conflicts; alienation (both social, religious and economic) and contradictions of modernity can be dealt with and pacified.

The conflict is spiritually and socially played publicly through spiritual rituals. This should not be reduced to a psychological phenomenon because these rituals are dealing with real life situations of alienation, personal and society disintegration and disenchantment.

Today's religious experiences being experienced in Zambia can be partly interpreted socially as a way of dealing with economic and social changes that have taken place through capitalism. Many people have been left socially, culturally vulnerable and disintegrated.

The contradictions include disparities in economic and social life. Some work very hard but still remain very poor while some live very luxurious lives without hard work. Some have been educated with degrees in their hands but these degrees have never given them any rewards.

Some have contracted high class marriages but without any fulfilment. These contradictions have to be dealt with within the context of African world-view and belief. The economic disparity is pushed into the religious realm for answers. People start to seek out alternative means and solutions.

Sometimes that may simply break from the norms and may even violate established norms and laws. This becomes an experience of disconnectedness and disenchantment from the means that allow people to achieve valued goals and promised modernity.

The available values, norms and expectations are seen as empty without meaning. This is the anomic space pointed out by Emile Durkheim and built on by Robert Merton through the structural strain theory.[180] The values which were in force before no longer hold any meaning for life.

However, structural strain theory cannot be limited to outcomes of crimes and deviance, but can go further to explain the search for meaning in the case of religious experiences. I would argue that structural strain does not only lead to crime and deviance as

---

[180] Halls W.D, trans., The Division of Labor in Society (New York: Simon and Schuster, 1997, (1897) and elaborated more the same concept in; John Spaulding, trans., Suicide: A study in Sociology (New York: The Free Press, 1979, (1897).

interpreted by sociologists at the level of the society.[181] Structural strains can lead to individual strains as well, which are frictions and pains experienced by an individual as one looks for ways to satisfy both material and spiritual needs.

This individual strain can also lead to spiritual emptiness as well. These strains are not just material in nature but can be spiritual as well because of lack of meaningful rituals to deal with them.

Traditional Christian Churches (Main Line Churches) fail to offer answers to the questions like those already alluded to above while prophetic and independent churches tackle such issues by tapping into the logic of traditional beliefs by weaving the threads of life and unlocking the human blessings in the web of relationships of people through rituals.

Some of these rituals appear irrational and deviance in nature but they make sense to the participants in search for meaning. Traditional or main line churches fail to break this populism of traditional orientation by shifting people to the religion of rationality and intellectualism.

This shift is unable to offer answers to questions of life of the people. Slowly the traditional and main line churches are challenged and losing out on the monopoly of the concept of normality and abnormality, evil and good.

Religious rituals become one way in which these hidden conflicts can be expressed and dramatized. This is falling back on the world of ideas, beliefs, illusions some of which appear irrational to the observer.

Religious ritual spaces have become spaces for social, spiritual, inner and economic healing. Ritual space is a space of healing individuals and society hoping for the social change that is desired through religion. This is acceptable to many because they are digging deep into the traditional beliefs embedded in the African world-view; importance of rituals.

The religious experiences we are witnessing today are an effort to make meaning in a conflictual environment between the infrastructure and the superstructure. It is an effort to recreate and reconstruct a new superstructure that will give answers to the altered relations of production. It is a yearning for a superstructure that

---

[181] Robert Merton, "Social Structure and Anomie", *American Sociological Review*, 3 (5): (1938), 672 – 682.

responds to the individual existential problems independent of scientific analysis. This calls for, in this case, visionary individuals who are creative able to bring together both old (traditional) and new symbols (Christian) through collective rituals.[182] This is the role being played today by many pastors, men of God, prophets and traditional healers. Rituals in this case become a resource for daily life, spiritually, socially and economically.

Many church members are not concerned about these new spiritual developments because they are answering to people's needs and aspirations. The ritual of revealing and to make visible the hidden realities is proving to be popular among the people through the prophets and men of God.

People who attend these church services of these prophets some belong to other traditional churches forgetting about what their churches teach. Membership to a church is not about what a particular church teaches (doctrine), but what it can offer in terms of meaningful rituals (instrumentalization of rituals).

Today it is a common phenomenon to find independent Christian churches without membership boundaries in form of conferences, spiritual rallies and of miracles. People flock to these conferences that are advertised on big bill-boards along the main roads and highways.

These have become Christian churches without boundaries of denomination and doctrine. This is typical of the nature of African traditional religions. They are religious traditions without boundaries. This is true also with traditional healers. Traditional healing rituals have no boundaries. Advertisements of traditional healers in Zambia clad the streets side by side with the Christian churches. Sometimes adverts are posted side by side.

They are interpreted as ritual alternatives to each other for the people. Here people can make a choice or they can choose both. Religious experience has become a commodity for commercialization or commoditization of religion.

The above shows the interconnectedness of rituals and African way of life. The growing and popularization of public rituals can also be viewed from the perspective of unfulfilled spiritual longing which has created a vacuum being filled by all manner of prophets, religious

---

[182] Win van Binsbergen, "Religious Innovation and political conflict in Zambia", (The Lumpa rising),
http://www.geocites.com/africanreligion/lumpa0.htm. Accessed on 25/02/2001.

charlatans and the wave of Pentecostal churches. This has problematized the notion of African rituals. While the so called prophets and new churches are tapping into African traditional religions understanding, they are also demonizing African rituals. There is the exploiting of African religiosity for commercial purposes.

Chapter 5

Religious Groups and African Life

Over the years Zambia has experienced a proliferation of religious groups and independent churches. Some have been break-a-ways from the main line traditional churches. Some of the church leaders of these break-a-ways have been schooled spiritually in the main line churches.

The main reason of breaking away from the traditional churches being that these leaders have been called sometimes through visions to do works for God, preach, and pray for people and to help their communities. To many observers this appears to be strange to hear.

Other reasons among many include misunderstanding on moral standing of some members, differences on interpretation of some teachings of the church, leadership wrangles, fighting over control of church resources and many other reasons, were some individuals have been expelled from some churches and form their own churches, there is also a popular belief in Christianity that the spirit of Jesus Christ can work through different people in different ways.

This theological understanding is extended even to the creation of churches. No one church has the monopoly of the spirit of God and the power of God cannot be confined only to a few churches.

5.1. Fragmentations of Religions in Africa

African traditional religious rituals have never had permanent or well-defined membership. To the contrary traditional Christian churches have registers and records of membership.

Traditional Christian churches count members by virtue of initiation and identification in their churches because everyone born in it is a member by birth. Initiation in African traditional life is for "growth in special knowledge" of traditions and not membership of one ritual group. According to traditional Christian churches once one is initiated into the Church, for example the Catholic Church, that individual cannot change the ritual affiliation. This is the same with Islam. But his is not the case with some African traditional religions, were one in certain circumstances can change one's ritual affiliation depending on needs and life challenges.

Plural religious ritual allegiance is something common in African traditional religions. An individual may become a member of more than one religious rituals even religious congregations or churches at the same time.

A Christian may even be practicing religious rituals that are regarded as incompatible with Christian belief and teaching.[183] This approach to religion makes Africa a fertile ground for different religions and different Christian expressions. Different religions are seen as built on different rituals which expresses a cultural orientation of African traditional religions.

Proliferation of churches is a common phenomenon in Africa. For example, there is no one ritual for healing in Africa in traditional setting. There are different rituals performed by different ritual leaders with different approaches. This is the context of African spirituality.

Sometimes different ritual leaders are specialized in different approaches to different challenges of society. Some are specialized in dealing and explaining deaths, while others in dealing with witchcraft and mental illnesses. Some in dealing with curses, wealth seeking and others in dealing with specific health issues. This indicates that African traditional religions gives different options of rituals dealing with what threatens human life. This same understanding is applied to Christian religion and its different approaches to human life.

5.2.   Ritual Leadership in African Traditional Religions

No ritual in African traditional religions can claim permanent membership of its clients like in Christian traditional churches where you even keep records of members. Membership is by birth and not by registration. When you are born in a particular cultural setting and group of people, you automatically become a member of that particular group of people.

Outsiders are free to be part of any ritual group if accepted. One is therefore, free to seek help of any ritual performance. Membership is based on what the ritual can offer. Rituals in African traditional

---

[183] Stephen Ellis and Gerrie ter Haar, Politics and African Religious Traditions, 175-201.

religions are performed at different levels by different ritual leaders. For example, at the level of a kingdom, certain rituals are performed by kings and chiefs on behalf of the people.

This is so because the king or the chief is seen as symbolic figure of cosmic order and stability. These leaders stand as embodiments of values of the kingdom. They can perform cleansing and fertility rites for their kingdoms.

At another level of a family, which in many African contexts is considered a "sacred institution" the eldest and depending on descent (matrilineal or matrilineal), takes up the spiritual role on behalf of the family. This can happen during birth of a child, name-giving, giving a blessing, marriage and death.

Then there are ritual leaders who are appointed and initiated through dreams by the spirits of the ancestors for the good of the general society. Their knowledge into the needs of the people come through dreams. Some are trained by other ritual leaders of the community.

They have power to diagnose different kinds of misfortunes and healing powers. These can be witch-finders, seers, diviners, prophets, guardians, fortune-tellers, shrine priests, among others. These are usually approached by those who need help on various needs.

They perform various rituals for the people from different backgrounds. Just as the West societies have different people playing different roles in their communities like social workers, psychologists, counsellors, ordained priests, medical doctors, traditional African societies prides in their different ritual leaders whom the Western religions and culture looks upon with scorn because of its dualistic thinking and approach to life.

Westerners sometimes fail to understand the powers of these traditional ritual leaders.[184] This is another nature of African traditional religions when it comes to ritual leadership.

It is something that is fragmentary in nature. At the centre of all these is the ritual performed to answer to the daily needs of the people.[185] People oscillate among all these ritual leaders depending on what they are looking for and their life challenges. This orientation may explain religious fragmentations as we experience them today in

---

[184] Jennifer Alt and Alison Munro, Ubuntu-Living: Being positive about people (Johannesburg: Catholic Psychological Services, 1997), 23 -25.

[185] John, S. Mbiti, Introduction to African Religion. 2nd ed. (Nairobi: East African Educational Publishers Ltd, 1990), 131 – 143.

Zambia. It is part of the nature of African traditional religions in accommodating different rituals groups at different times in the same society.

Rituals are actions which are wrapped in a web of symbolisms with different meanings for participants. These are patterned behaviour consisting of prescribed actions performed periodically and / or repetitively. A ritual has a power to communicate some hidden meaning on different human experiences. Behind every ritual action there is a purpose, function and meaning.

Different actions in a ritual communicate different things to different people. People participate in a ritual for specific purpose and the ritual serves as an instrument of a specific function to give a specific meaning in a given circumstance.[186]

Many African traditional rituals have no boundaries. This gives a sense why some Africans understand their conversion to Christianity not as a revolution or big change, a fundamental break with tradition. For some, Christian ritual is just another ritual among many other rituals one can approach at different times in life.

Proliferations of independent and prophetic churches are an enlargement of the available ritual possibilities and choices which is something very positive for an African.

This is destructive to a Western theologian who does not understand the logic of practice of African traditional religions. This is how dynamic and structural openness of African traditional religions can be. It is a very accommodative religion.

Ritual duality is part of African Traditional Religions and practices. Evidence abounds today in many African societies about Africans who continue to hold beliefs derived from traditional cosmologies and applying them to their daily lives and activities.

This is in spite of living in modern cities and involved in modern life.[187] New religious institutions are introduced, borrowed from elsewhere or invented according to the expanding needs of the society. Participants in different rituals can come from different cultural backgrounds and settings. Rituals of healing, cleansing, divination and many other crisis rituals have no static membership. Participants can come from across languages, nationalities and tribal

---

[186] David Kertzer, Ritual, Politics and Power (London: Yale University Press, 1988), 9.

[187] Stephen Ellis and Gerrie ter Haar, Politics and African Religious Traditions, 175-201.

boundaries. What is important in a ritual is the meaningfulness that it gives to the lived experience.

Religious changes and experiences are related to social changes in the way of life of society, contacts with other peoples, new needs and aspirations that are emerging today by the greatly expanded scale of the world in order to cope with new situations.

This is evident from the proliferation of Apostles and prophetic churches across Africa. Today we have mega churches in African towns and cities with no definable membership. Membership is across Africa. This makes a ritual to be the basis of order of society.

A ritual is able to constrain people from engaging in activities that are not compatible with social order of which they are members. Rituals are capable of softening the emotional state of a human being through dance, music, drugs, visual aids and minds in return are engraved with concepts or notions to which an individual becomes attached strongly.

This makes a ritual a powerful instrument of dealing with contradictions in human life. A ritual is able to deal with the speculative world-view in a more practical way. A ritual therefore, defines the social and natural world of a human being and society through compulsive concepts like health, prosperity and fruitfulness, security and protection.

Rituals are not merely expressive but they are pragmatic actions which affect the transformation of the world. They help to construct meaningfulness of the immediate world.

A meaningful ritual is one that is able to fuse together the world as lived and the world as imagined (mythical) through symbolic actions and brings about transformation in one's sense of reality. People participate in a ritual for the purpose of what Clifford Geertz calls enactments, materializations and realizations.[188] An African is free to abandon a ritual that does not make sense of the lived world and participate in another ritual that makes sense.

For example, the ritual of confession in the Catholic Church in Zambia is almost dying. Perhaps, it is because the questions of materializations and realizations are not being met in the life of the people.

---

[188] Clifford Geertz, The Interpretation of Cultures (London: Fontana Press, 1973), 113 - 114.

May be this sacrament does not give answers to the inner quests of many people. It is a ritual that has become remote to the life solutions of the people in their search for meaningful daily life. There is nothing to compel people to this ritual anymore.

Therefore, old rituals may die while new ones come on the religious scene. This explains the emergence of thousands and thousands of Independent Churches and new religious groups in Africa and Zambia in particular. It also sheds light on the ease with which Zambians pass from one church to another.

The religious rituals in some of these religious groups are not clearly defined like rituals found in Christian traditional churches. There is a lot of what I can term as "religious shopping", moving from church to church and no one finds it wrong because it is something embedded in African religions.

Most of the religious groups sprouting in Zambia are characterized by easy fragmentations. Break –a-ways and formation of new religious groups is a common phenomenon. This can be argued that this follows the traditional characteristic of traditional ritual groups that are fragmentary in nature and some may not even be permanent.

Religious groups in Zambia have a characteristic of fragmenting for different reasons, ranging from power play, ritual emphasis, seeking prosperity, in need of more charismatic approaches to Christianity, to visionary and prophetic messages to individuals in their congregations, sexual scandals, fraudulency and some are banned by the government for breaking the state laws.

In traditional Christian churches members who are not happy with the spirituality in their congregations where they belong, are free to change their congregations and congregate with another group of their choice or even being a member of different ritual group all together. Sometimes people fall back on the fundamentals of Christianity in a fundamentalist way as response and reaction to the watering down of what they believe.

5.3. Christian Fundamentalism and African Traditional Religions

In the late 1970s to the early 1990s, the Zambian society was religiously influenced by Christian fundamentalism, mostly from America. This was a rigid adherence to Christian doctrines for their own sake. While we can look at Christian fundamentalism as wave of the 19th Century across the globe, it has to be mentioned that Christian fundamentalism is found in all religious groups, protestants, Catholic, Jewish and Islam.

Fundamentalism is the appealing to doctrine in literal sense than to the spirit of doctrine. It is the interpretation of belief, doctrine, scripture, Koran among others, in a literal way. It is the shaping of the teaching to one's or a group point of view in the name of religion.

Therefore, fundamentalism may not be shared by the whole body of a religious group. Such people with such orientations are found in all religions. It has to be pointed out that fundamentalism was a reaction to the 19th Century ideas that threatened the Christian traditions and doctrines with the new explanations of reality through the evolutionary theory by Charles Darwin and Thomas Huxley.

They proposed the theory of different species of organisms coming into existence and developing into higher creatures at different times. This implies that all that exists come not from the immediate creation of God, but descended from one another including the human being, coming from an ape millions of years ago.

This was the taking away of authority of study of human beings and creation from theology and bringing it into the area of natural history and science.[189] This was interpreted as a rejection of God as the creator of the material and immaterial worlds. The idea was pushing God out of the equation of creation and control of natural order.

It implied that man could live without belief in God. Embracing such a theory is antithetical to the faith and existence of God.

Then there was development of psychoanalysis by Sigmund Freud which espoused that God is a merely human wishful thinking. There was no such authority as God who wants a human being to behave in a certain way. Belief in God is an indication of infantile approach to seeking security and problem solving in the creation of "God".

This development led to deconstruction of absolute truth about human life. There is no one way of approaching reality. The principle of absolutism was challenged. Principle of relativity took centre stage in the analysis of life. It supported the different approaches to some truths and human realities. This led to defined relative morality and

---

[189] Charles Darwin, The Origin of Species. 6th ed. (London: John Murray, 1872), 146 – 156. First published in 1859; Thomas, Huxley, Man's place in Nature and Other Essays (London: Macmillan, 1894).

actions like homosexuality, same sex marriages, abortion, threatening the morality taught by Christian religion which find its source in absoluteness of Supreme Being (God).[190]

It led to the disavowing of any absolute universal moral standards. This development promoted the principle of relativism, questioning of objective truth and promotion of secularization. Christianity saw secularization as being practically synonymous with atheism with its promotion of practical materialism and humanism.

A human being becomes, according to Christianity, an end in himself, the sole maker, with supreme control of his own history and destiny. This saw a significant decline in the significance of religion, especially in public life. Religion was and is partly seen as a private and personal matter which should not find expression in the public domain.[191]

Friedrich Nietzsche, earlier talked about the theory of transvaluation of all values. This theory held that there are no absolute values and that holding of absolute values is resentment against life.

Holding God as an absolute value hinders human free realization and human responsibility in the world. In this case belief in God is a hindrance to self-human actualization. Nietzsche therefore declared, "God as dead" to free human beings from the clutches and claws of an imaginary God. For Nietzsche, this declaration meant the opening of new era in which Christian ethics will be replaced by life affirming philosophy.

God will no longer be a goal and sanction of human conduct.[192] A human being can live without the notion of God as a dictate of human values on life. Religion is held by its very nature as something that thwarts human emancipation by raising man's hopes in the future life. In this way religion becomes a deception and discouraging a human being from working for a better form of life in the present.

The theory of Karl Marx had as well earlier explained away religion as an empty consolation and a justification of an evil world - "religion as opium of the people". For Marx religion therefore, does not make man but man makes religion as a fantasy and a disease.

Marx and Engels being functionalists, they see and make religion as tool to make the society going. Religion for them is irrational

---

[190] Sigmund Freud, Totem and Tabu (Harmondsworth, 1938), 222 – 225.
[191] Catholic Church Catechism, 2124.
[192] Samuel E. Stumpf, Socrates to Sartre: A History of Philosophy. 3rd ed. (New York: McGraw-Hill Book Company, 1982), 358

because the object of its worship is not real and not a material reality. Religion just makes people to be docile to the status quo.[193]

As a reaction within Protestantism, it gave rise to Christian fundamentalism against modernism, materialism and its conciliatory tendencies towards scientific theories, which mainly involves holding strictly to doctrines or fundamentals. This, however, does not have its origin from Africa, but from the West, especially, America.

Traditional Christianity was endangered by the new developments in science and philosophy. African traditional religions being very open by nature, embraced Christian fundamentalism as another alternative Christian expression, though today it is not as attractive as Christianity of prosperity which is a new development.

This shift cast a doubt on the importance of well-defined and systematic doctrine in traditional Christian religions. Africans embrace other Christian orientations, expressions and practices, not because there is something wrong with African traditional beliefs. African traditional religions are religions with alternative expressions and thus are open religions. The spread of Christian fundamentalism in Zambia, for example, was not necessarily based on the perception of threat to Christian doctrine in Africa or on African traditional religions.

Christian fundamentalism came in just as another alternative religious ritual trying to give answers to life questions. Africa is a fertile ground for new expressions of different religions because of the nature of its culture and its religious dispositions.

Today it is being said that Islam is one of the most popular growing religions in Africa. This is not only in its traditional territories (East, North and West Africa) but even outside these territories.

For example, Islam is on the rise in Rwanda. One of the strong points of Islam is that it is accommodative of the local cultures it encounters to an extent that some scholars have argued that Islam is a traditional African religion.[194] This is so because Islam is being accommodated with easy by African people just as they did with Christianity in the past. The reason is that it is giving answers to life

---

[193] Karl Marx – F. Engels, On Religion (Atlanta: Schochen Books, 1964), 41.
[194] http://africanholocaust.net/islamafrica/islam-and-africa/. Accessed on 11/23/2017. https://en.wikipedia.org/wiki/islam_in_Africa. Accessed on 11/24/2017.

challenges among Africans. It has come as an alternative to different African religious expressions.

5.4. Doctrine and African Belief Systems

From a Western point of view, one of the characteristics of a religion is the body of "well defined, systematic, coherent and articulated doctrines". Please take note that this discourse is not disputing the existence of doctrines in African traditional religions, but a well-defined, systematic, coherent and articulated doctrine.

That is in reference to what a particular religious group teaches and believes in and passes on to its members and the newly converted. However, it has to be mentioned that it is not in all religions that you will find well defined body of doctrines that govern the members.

The interactions of African traditional religions with its adherents have to be interpreted partly from this angle of absence of refined, systematic and coherent doctrine. African traditional religions are more pragmatic centred than doctrinally oriented. African traditional religions are more in practical life as it is lived than just an intellectual thing.

African traditional religions are not more in the academics as compared to traditional and missionary Christianity. African traditional religions are more in life as lived than head knowledge.

Most of the Traditional African Religions do not have well defined and coherent doctrines that members follow. They may have beliefs about certain aspects like the supreme - being, ancestors, spiritual possession, creation and its origins, importance of names etc. However, just as Neckebrouck explains, there is no body of defined teachings which is systematic, well-articulated, harmoniously integrated and coherent or something we can call a theology of religion as we have it in Christianity and other world religions.

Though there may be something close to some doctrine, it is not necessarily a common one for all members of a given religious group. It is not also considered as important for all members to hold the same doctrine.[195] African Traditional Religions do not demand adherence to any single doctrine as a proof of being a member of African traditional Religions.

---

[195] Valeer Neckebrouck, The Nature of African Traditional Religion.

The focus of African traditional religions is above all practical and not just head knowledge and loyalty to some set of packaged doctrine to be accepted. Doctrines in African thought systems are "written" in music, traditional songs, dances, and poetry, proverbs, storytelling, art and ritual performances.[196] These serve as cultural and religious books for an African.

These books are not kept on bookshelves in academic libraries. They are kept in minds, hearts and bodies. These libraries are embodied and engraved in bodies and life experiences.

Even the change of membership from one ritual to another is not based on the acceptability of a well-defined body of doctrines. Change of ritual group is based on expressive and instrumental aspects of rituals.

If one ritual is not effective, one is free to go and join and participate in another one. This explains the polarization that exists among different religious groups in Zambia.

One can belong to more than one church because an African can participate in more than one ritual depending on how aspirations, needs and challenges of life may be met. Today, one can consult a different ritual performed by a different ritual leader and can again consult a different one the following week or continue to consult both. To a participant in ritual, this is not a contradiction at all.

To many Zambians, churches are seen in terms of rituals and not based on different doctrines. While there is an appreciation of doctrine, but most importantly the ritual occupies the centre of spiritual life. Preoccupation is not with doctrine but the performance and participation in the ritual. The ritual is the heart of religion for a Zambian.

In some cases, scandalous pastors (sexual scandals in their congregations, luxury scandalous lives, financial frauds and misappropriation of congregational funds) are tolerated as long as the ritual they perform is effective for the followers. These are issues based on doctrines and teaching and not rituals. This argument about the importance of ritual over doctrine in certain religions like African traditional religions is old in anthropology.

In African setting meaning of life is transmitted through the daily experiences of life. Abstract concepts are not very fundamental.

---

[196] Chris Nwaka Egbulem, "African Spirituality", The New Dictionary of Catholic Spirituality, 19.

What is important is search and discovery of meaning of life through participation of each member in the collective experience with others and life. This is where rituals become important.[197]

Robertson Smith who is known as a "ritualist" in anthropology argued that ritual is central to religion than doctrine, though he approached rituals with a sense of degradation in the expression of religion. According to Smith, rituals are the heart of religion.

There is no religion without a ritual. He considered rituals to be materialistic in nature only disguised under the clock of mysticism. Therefore, for Smith rituals are indicators of barbaric and uncivilized cultures. He saw those religions dominated by ritual, as lower on the evolutionary scale than the religions of morality like Christianity, Islam, Judaism, among others, though many may not agree with him on this. There is no known religion that is devoid of aspects of morality or even ritual.

Every religion has an aspect of ritual that plays as part of centrality of religion. Therefore, for smith to say that rituals are indicators of barbarism and not being civilized does do sound true. Every religion has a moral orientation at some level though this may not be very amplified or seen as central. For African Traditional religions since it permeates all realms of life, morality in every aspect of African life is cardinal.

However, we can agree with Robertson Smith when he points out that the idea of belief, doctrine, dogma as being important for understanding of religion than ritual is a mistake that springs from the dogmatic approach of the main traditional religions like Christianity, Islam and Jewish, especially in the context of African traditional religions.

This makes these "book religions" blind to the reality of other religions.[198] Today many anthropologists think of religion as constituted or caused by ritual than myths and doctrines. It is in the ritual that people experience the reinforcement of life, fertility, communion with the Supreme Being and power.

---

[197] Martin Nkafu Nkemnkia, African Vitalogy: A step forward in African thinking, 109.

[198] Robertson Smith (1846 – 1894) was a Scottish Presbyterian theologian, with specialization in the Old Testament Studies but later came to anthropology, wrote several works, but two of his works stand out distinctly on this subject of importance of ritual over doctrine: Kinship and Marriage in Early Arabia (1885) and Lectures on the Religion of the Semites (1889).

Today anthropologists agree that rituals are the most important part or aspect of most religions. They form the heart and the core of religion. Death of a religion comes in with the deserting of rituals.

A very good example is the popularity of open-air performances of healing and night prayer sessions by religious leaders, who may be both international and local, in Zambia. Most Zambians attend and participate in these public healing rituals by different churches and denominations regardless of which church one belongs to.

Attendance is not based on the teachings of the churches people belong to but simply on the ritual and what they expect to experience from it. It is a common experience in Zambia that when one visits a place where one cannot find one's traditional church; some people attend and go to other churches that are available with ease.

They give a simple reason for doing that. They would say "we all believe in one God". Many Zambians are not concerned with a systematic and a logically coherent set of doctrines but they are concerned with ritual techniques which respond to their meaningful world. This is true not only for Zambians but for many African people.

It is a common experience in many Catholic Church communities that many Catholics do not pay attention to instructions (Doctrine) in order to receive the church Sacraments. This is one of the pre-conditions to receive any Sacrament in the Catholic Church. One cannot be allowed to receive any Sacrament without instructions.

The purpose of this condition is to make the recipients understand what they are receiving and be schooled in the Catholic faith. The experience and reality in some situations attest to the fact that many would like to receive and do receive the Sacraments even without being instructed. Some do receive sacraments in the Catholic Church without being instructed in the doctrines of the Catholic Church.

And in many instances, the instructions are very poorly conducted to prepare someone for the reception of Church sacraments. Even some priests do not see this as important, their attention is on dispensing the sacraments. It will be interesting to find out how Christian independent churches that have mash-roomed over the years how they prepare their converts, let us say, for their rituals like baptism if they do practice them.

Do they have coherent doctrines to change the thinking or the way of life of the people as they become new converts? This western approach to doctrine in order to understand religious beliefs of particular denominations is a challenge to many African logic of practice.

Attention is paid to receiving the sacraments and participation in the ritual and not understanding the sacraments. In some churches, even outside the Catholic Church, people are baptized in huge numbers without introduction to the main doctrines of their Churches if they have any.

Even those who are instructed in the doctrines of particular religious' groupings, it is not a guarantee that they will not cross the religious ritual boundaries in the future.

In the early to the late 1930s, the White Fathers in their study of the local customs and traditions among the Bemba people of Northern Province of Zambia had put it clearly when they said:

> It would be a serious mistake to assume that pagan customs are rapidly disappearing; this unfortunately, is far from being the case. In all sincerity we must admit that heretofore our efforts in this direction have been rather lacking, and this has been due to our lack of a complete knowledge of these customs. Let us not be simple- minded than we need to be. We have a good number of catechumens preparing for baptism and other similar groups, who solemnly declare that they have abandoned all pagan practices; but the fact remains that in a good many cases, they have not, in reality, done so.[199]

The early missionaries had seen how deeply rooted the local people were in their traditional practices. Their project was to know the culture in order to convert them to the new religion. It would be interesting to know why they had seen their evangelizing mission to be such a mammoth task among the Babemba people.

Why was this doubt brought out so strongly? In the same monograph, it is pointed out why a Native Christian is unable to see the uselessness of such practices (traditional practices) – Native customs are part and parcel of life. The Native practices constitute a

---

[199] Native Customs: A study of the Babemba and neighbouring tribes, unknown year of publication, 1. This was a study and collection of traditional and cultural practices among the BaBemba people by the White Fathers. The White Fathers were among the earliest missionaries to enter the Northern part of Zambia. This study was directed by the Conference of the Ordinaries of Rhodesia and Nyasaland through the Apostolic Delegate Monsignor Riberi held at Chilubula in 1934.

perfectly rational and logical system in its own way different from Christianity.[200] This is a clear indication of defeat and how deeply an African is rooted in the local culture, how mistaken and misplaced the western missionary approach was.

At the same time, there is acceptance of local logic of practice and rationality from an African point of view. This exposition by the early missionaries is something to look at when we are analysing the spiritual and religious experiences we are experiencing today in Zambia.

Being and participating in the ritual is more important than the doctrine and understanding the ritual. Eades found the same among the Yoruba people of West Africa. The belief in the efficacy of rituals is more important than a systematic doctrine. For many Africans, religion deals greatly with challenges of individuals in their life and not the systematic doctrine.[201]

One of the most important aspects to indicate the importance of rituals does not lie in the convictions of the doctrines (instructions) but in the testimonies (religious experiences) of the people who participate in the rituals. Sometimes, and in certain circumstances, one's testimonies would even contradict the doctrines.

This contradiction may not be taken as a serious issue by the participants in the ritual. The testimonies are not meant to validate the doctrines of a particular religious group. The testimonies indicate the efficacy of the ritual performed. This is a challenge to a Western theological mind. Usually, it is the ritual and the context in which it is performed that determines the way of a religion and not the contents of doctrines.

Therefore, when we are looking at some of the religious experiences in African religions and the religious experiences in Zambia' society today in particular, it is important not to exaggerate the expectations of the influence of a logical consistency and coherence of Christian belief systems (Doctrine). For many participants that is not a cardinal point.

---

[200] Ibid., 1.
[201] J.S. Eades, The Yoruba Today (Cambridge: Cambridge University Press, 1980), 128.

The point is ritual performance and participation in it though this may not be applicable to all Africans. There are some who put emphasis on belief overshadowing the component of a ritual.[202]

Wilson argues differently about the Western Christianity, he says that, when the interpretation of the truths of religion become too remote from the people's everyday circumstances and experiences, people cease to support such a religion.

This is what has happened to Christianity in the West. The structures, doctrines and teachings and its bureaucratic approach have overshadowed the real experiences of the people. Wilson continues to argue that when religious teachings become obscure and the conditions for salvation too remote, followers of such religious groups seek recourse to alternative sources of reassurance and to other avenues of reaching out to the supernatural.[203] This salvation is not only in the future (eschatological), it is salvation in the now and present life and daily experiences, of illnesses, misfortunes, poverty, bad luck, etc.

This is true in the context of Western religion and not African traditional religions. Wilson relates truths (doctrine) to life which is not usually the case for Africans. Very few Africans change or shift from one church to another because of conflict with doctrines.

Change of ritual or switching to another ritual may not necessarily be based on doctrine and remoteness of eschatological salvation but the giving of meaning to their present life, desires, inner and social conflicts, needs, aspirations and alienation from modernity and progress. Few Africans change their ritual because of doctrine. On many occasions, they make a shift based on meaningfulness of a ritual to daily life and its impact on the material life of people.

However, this indicates the active role of an African in the process of conversion. An African is not passive human person but remains a protagonist in the religious experiences.

An African is able to determine whether to accept any religious invitation or not and which aspects are acceptable or not. At the same

---

[202] Mathias Guenther, Tricksters and Trancers: Bushman Religion and Society (Bloomington: Indiana University Press, 1999), 59.

[203] Bryan Wilson, Religion in Sociological Perspective (Oxford: Oxford University Press, 1982), 122. Salvation here has to be understood as life of liberation from social, political, religious, economic and psychological chains. Salvation for an African is not only in the future (eschatological) but it embraces the present life with its challenges. Salvation is not only something spiritual but material as well.

time an African determines how to combine what is religiously acceptable with the practices one adheres to. Such integration sometimes, of strange elements from other religious groups, is not something new. An African is a person of practical rituals that give meaning to daily experiences.

5.5. Syncretism as a Euro-Christian Conflict

Syncretism is a reference to the practicing or combining of two or more different beliefs. It can be defined as an amalgamation or hybridization of two or more cultural belief systems. For Christianity this is not acceptable. Christianity preaches the leaving behind of all the lived past and embracing the new life in Christ. One becomes a born again in living, beliefs, habits, attitudes and general way of life.

Therefore, for Christianity one cannot live double lives, living the old and embracing the new, holding on to an old belief and embracing a new one at the same time. This is what syncretism is. Christianity taught to Africans by the missionaries had a fear of syncretism. Christianity wanted to keep itself "pure" from other beliefs.[204]

Christian conversion is a complete break away from one kind of life into the new. It is from this definition that syncretism derives its negative connotation from a Christian point of view. In African traditional religions there is no concept of conversion as understood in Western Christianity. One cannot be converted to African religion.

It has no orientation or an aspect of converting others to follow. An African instead is born in the religion of African traditions which does not need conversion. What is needed is initiation into life of an African. One becomes part of this religion through socialization, participation, initiations, practices of rituals and life experiences.

African religion is within life itself and not something one comes to take up at some point in life after breaking away from some lived experiences. Even participating in another ritual does not require necessarily one to go under, well defined, articulated and systematic doctrines like in Christianity or other religions. Through-out one's life one is just introduced to the deeper understanding of practices, symbolisms, rituals and life as it is supposed to be lived.

---

[204] Jesse Mugambi, Critique of Christianity in African Literature (Nairobi: Heineman, 1992), 60.

Christianity does not believe in the emerging of two or more religious belief systems with different rituals in the life of a convert. It has to be however, appreciated and noted that the African Christian converts do combine their new found religious beliefs and practices with beliefs and practices of their traditional religions and beliefs.

This practice traditionally is what is called "syncretism". It is perceived in a rather very pejorative and negative way by Western Christianity. Theologians and missiologists consider it as an evidence of corrupting what is known as "pure Christian religion". Many theologians have considered this approach of Africans to life as "primitive" or "pre-logical" mentality.

Syncretism in this context has a very negative pejorative connotation from a Western perspective. It is something very negative in Western Christian logical and thought system but not for an African. Mushindo, one of the prolific Zambian writers with deep roots in Zambian history, African intellectual heritage and philosophical appreciation, rejects out rightly the idea that African cultural beliefs make Africans undisposed and unfit for Christianity, which was the approach of missionaries. He argues against the idea that Africans to become Christians had to discard their traditional beliefs and values. His position is that Africans did not need to renounce their cultural belief systems in order to be Christians.[205]

It is this approach of Western religion which led to condemnation of many African traditions and practices which, today is seen to be a regrettable approach. Western Christian religion was and is still bent on keeping itself "pure and uncorrupted". World religions for a long time have had this approach of "conquering" the "other".

This is interpreted in the context of modernization or progress theories which believed in the diffusion of Western modernization from the centre of the world (Europe) to the periphery (traditional societies).

Western religion was seen as part of the whitening of traditional, backward minds and the Dark Continent. Christianity as part of the modernization project was considered as a spiritual and social instrument to bring about social change in morality and cultural values of traditional societies.

---

[205] Ackson M. Kanduza, "Towards a History of Ideas in Zambia", (ed.) Samuel N. Chipungu, *Guardians in their time: Experience of Zambians under Colonial Rule, 1890 – 1964*, (London: The Macmillan Press LTD, 1992), 132 -133.

Christianity was considered in itself as an advanced culture and other cultures different from it as "primitive" and "backwards", damned and in need of salvation. Traditional cultures and practices were considered as obstacles to civilization, modernization, development and to the new Christian religion.

This approach to African cultures is still rife and much alive even by priests and pastors whose minds have been whitened by European religious human formation and education. This has made enculturation just for seminars and theological discussions in many parts of Africa.

The fear of syncretism by the Western traditional Churches was deeply entrenched in their cultural approach to other religions. Other religions were seen with the spectacles of suspicion and scepticism. It has to be mentioned that African religion has a different scenario when it comes to the amalgamation of different belief systems. Africa has had examples of people who have integrated Christianity with other indigenous religious traditions. [206]

Nkwame Nkrumah, the first president of Ghana declared himself a Marxist-Leninist and a non-denominational Christian. Nkrumah never saw any contradiction in this amalgamation without identifying himself with one religious ritual.[207]

Many of the Christian mega churches that are developing in Africa have this orientation of non-denominational approach. There are churches were Catholics, Protestants, Christian fundamentalists, non-Christians and other church members can attend freely and comfortably without any qualms of conscience.

These mega churches are usually full of people who attend the services. Some are called churches for all nations, synagogues, Temples or with different names that carry a sense of inclusivity and non-denominational. This is a clear tapping in the African logic, belief and mode of African ritual.

It can be attested that millions of African Muslims and Christians still absorb from their African belief systems values and beliefs which are retained in their new found religions. Belonging to different rituals at the same time does not bring any discomfort or shame to

---

[206] Katerina Mildnerova, "African Independent Churches in Zambia (Lusaka)", Ethnologia Actualis, Vol. 14, No. 2, (2014). content.sciendo.com. Accessed on 24.02.2021.

[207] Nkwame Nkrumah, Ghana: The autobiography of Nkwame Nkrumah (Edinburgh and New York: Nelson, 1957)

an African.[208] African context is a context of different rituals performed at different times for different circumstances and sometimes by different figures in the community.

Rituals can be performed at different levels, domestic home, extended family, community of different families and ethnic group. One can join any ritual depending on needs and the returns a particular ritual offers.

After the considerations and accounts, we have already made on ritual and doctrine in regard to African traditional Religions, "syncretistic" behaviour becomes very clear as part of life for an African. This can be considered as the logical and natural outcome of the pragmatic and non-doctrinaire approach of African traditional religions. African traditional religion is a practical religion based on what people yearn for in their practical life and what they desire. It is a religion that is lived in practical terms and daily life.

Theoretical concepts are not very central to African religious life. And systematic and coherent doctrine is not very fundamental and critical to the religious experience and the African people's desires.

It means therefore, that the question as to which elements of the traditional religions have to be retained and which ones have to be dropped, depends not so much on the constraints of systematic or coherent and integrated theological constructs, but on the needs, necessities, functionalities, teleology, utilities and demands of the secular situation here and now and its inherent dynamics. This is what is important for an African.

Raphael Ndingi Mwana'a Nzeki, the former Archbishop of Nairobi acknowledged and regretted the existence of traditional African religious beliefs operating beneath the surface when they seemed to have been uprooted when he talked about (Christian) relations with other religions.[209]

This is a regret on the part of the former Archbishop about syncretism in the African Catholic Church today even after more than 100 years of existence of Catholic Christian faith in Africa. Christianity has failed to root out traditional beliefs and practices that are incompatible with Christianity.

---

[208] Ali A. Mazrui, The African Condition: A political Diagnosis, 54.
[209] Raphael S. Ndingi Mwana'a Nzeki, in "Identifying Challenges and Priorities in a Pastoral Approach to Culture in Africa", Pontificium Consilium de Cultura, *Handing on the Faith at the heart of Africa's Cultures* (2003), 89 – 90.

It should not be over-looked that African religion is not an intellectual religion based on metaphysical concepts. By this fact the argument is not that African religion is unreasonable or lacks intellectual element, but that intellectual concepts are not at the centre of African religion. If anything, these intellectual concepts are interpreted in the African complex way of life and religious experiences.

"Syncretism" in this approach with its negative connotation then is not on the part of the new converts but on the part of new-found Christian religion. Africans do not see "syncretism" in their approach when they combine Christianity and their traditional practices.

One is able to make a choice about which ritual appeals more to one's aspirations, needs and the crisis of the moment. For an African combining different rituals from different backgrounds is not perceived as syncretism with a negative connotation as we have it in Western Christianity. Therefore, syncretism as a concept in African traditional religions does not exist. The same connotation of the concept of syncretism from a Western point of view has made to approach even positive elements of African religion to be painted negative.

This combining of Christian and African Traditional beliefs occurs even among the religious leaders of Christian Traditional Churches. One experience comes to mind how one Catholic priest, who has gone through priestly formation, with high academic trails, served for a good number of years in the ministry and exposed to the macro-world would still believe and use coarse-salt by spreading it around his residential house to wad-off bad spirits and keep his enemies at bay.

A well and trusted pastor by his congregation with power to heal and perform miracles still goes to consult a diviner when in crisis. These are custodians of Christian rituals and doctrine, but still fall back on the African traditional rituals and beliefs. Kwesi Yankah and John Mbiti argue that many African peoples today have what can be termed as "mixed religious heritage", the reconciling of African traditional religions with the Abrahamic and Christian faiths. This is not problematic to an African but to a foreign missionary and Western Christian theologian.[210]

---

[210] Peek Philip M, Kwesi Yankah, "African Folklore", in *an Encyclopedia* (Taylor and Francis Press, 2004); John, Mbiti, Introduction to African Religion, 5.

Syncretism for many Africans is not as negative aspect as the Westerners may see it. Both Christianity and African traditional religions can be considered as alternatives for daily life depending on a situation of many Africans. One can choose which ritual to fall on in a given context. The conflict of syncretism with Christian values is not in the mind of an African but in the Christian conception of its religious values. For an African syncretism is an expression of alternatives available for life and not a double life.

In some practical ways, fundamentalism, ritual leadership, syncretism and their authority shade some light on the religious experiences in Zambia today. At the same time, it shows how powerful African traditional religions impact on African spirituality.

Chapter 6

Domestication of Christian Symbols

One of the representations of religious beliefs in African traditional religions is the belief that certain material objects, which may be either man-made or natural may be endowed with special powers (consecrated or animated) that can work to the advantage of the people. The energy or power that exists in the interaction between the visible and the invisible realities can be trapped and disseminated by ritual leaders to other people through objects, words and actions.[211]

Sometimes the use of an object with power is accompanied by actions and words (incantations). The Western philosophy described such objects held by Africans as fetish, amulets and talismans.

A Fetish to be described as such demands explicit statement that a spirit is considered as embodied in it, or acting through it, or communicating through it. Originally the term fetish referred to amulets [212] (feitico) carried by Portuguese sailors in the early days of European exploration.

Later the term was used by the Europeans for any object that they saw being used by the inhabitants of Africa in connection with what they considered magic.

---

[211] Damian, Kanuma, Musonda, Theological Reflections on Inculturation. http://www.jctr.org.zm/inculturation.htm. Accessed on 4/01.2001.

[212] The terms "amulet" and "Talisman" come from Arabic. Amulet is derived from the term "hamila", meaning "pendant". It is considered as an object protecting against spells or misfortune. According to Marie Cofta (Love One Another, 2017, No. 38), an amulet is usually a small object, natural or artificial, serving the purpose of magical protection against evil spirits, people or misfortune. It is worn on the body or under or on clothes, rings, figurines, chains, etc. A talisman is from an Arabic word called "tilasm" meaning the same as amulet. The difference between an amulet and a talisman is by function they fulfil. An amulet plays a protective role by warding off evil spirits and hostile powers. A talisman has the ability to ensure general happiness and luck in all kinds of endeavours. A talisman is produced by a sorcerer to satisfy a specific need. A good example of talismans is those rings Seer 1 alleged to have given some Zambian political leaders. Both amulets and talismans are charged with spiritual energy. According to Cofta all these are part of what is called primitive religion based on folk piety and superstition.

In this way a fetish has no exact meaning, but usually a manufactured object that is entered by spirits or impersonal powers after an appropriate ritual has been performed. From a European point of view, a fetish carries a negative connotation. Fetishes are used magically and are usually believed to be for protection, causing harm, bringing fortunes, or good health.

Fetishes are energy-giving substances which includes stones, horns, claws of birds and animals, teeth, bones, beads, hair, animal skin or any pieces of material, among others.[213] This brings out the concept of fetishes in African traditional religions. The term fetish has evolved from describing type of objects created in the interaction between European travellers and Africans. It is now considered as an analytical term that plays a central role in the perception of an African by a European.

Fetish as a concept was elaborated to demonize the supposedly arbitrary attachment of West Africans and Africans in general to material objects believed to animate some spiritual powers.

These received a very strong disapproval by Christianity of such objects as animism and suspicions.[214] Fetishism was seen by Christianity as fostering a shift of attention away from the relationship between people and God and focus instead on the relationship between people and material objects, leading to a fake model of causality of natural events.

The Western Christianity saw fetishes as replacing the place of God, a sin against the first commandment; "you shall not make yourself an idol…" In many African traditional religions, these fetishes never replaced the Supreme Being but served as instruments and medium of communication between the real world and the supernatural world.

A fetish was considered by a Westerner as evidence for the inherently backward, superstitious state of the African mind. A fetish in this way became stigmatized as something evil and unchristian.

Fetishism became synonymous with magic and pagan religion according to Christianity. Fetishism to a Western mind implied lack of capacity of an African for higher rationalization and worshiping of objects. In fact, what was not appreciated was the fact that African

---

[213] Klaus E. Muller and Ute, Ritz-Muller, Soul of Africa, Magical Rites and Traditions, 485-486.
[214] Stallybrass Peter in Daniel, Miller, Conception: Critical concepts in the social science (London: Routledge, 2001)

system of worship reflects a completely different system of rationalization.

Africans would define a "fetish", as a different form of expression of prayer which is translated into material form. It is therefore, making of a prayer more tangible than an intellectual thing of the mind only. The idol worship notion in this case becomes a Eurocentric interpretation. The tension between the Christian rational faith and practical faith still exists in the expression of Christianity.

An African instead has used the very symbols of Christian expression of faith like African traditional symbols which are animated with power to influence everyday life. This process is termed as domestication of Christian symbols by African traditional religions. Christian symbols are accepted not for what they mean in Christianity but for the local and cultural meaning that has been attached to them.

6.1. Anointing Oils, Holy Water and Christian Sacred Instruments

Today, there are certain symbolisms of Christianity that have been domesticated into fetishes in their use. We are seeing the proliferation of the mystical use of holy water, anointing oils, rosaries and crosses and other sacred and religious symbols.

These in a way are considered to animate in themselves religious and spiritual powers once they are consecrated or blessed by a man of God, a prophet or a priest. These have become popular religious symbols with power to protect, heal, bring good luck, and influence human events and other personal purposes and intentions.

To many it is not a question of using these symbols as Christianity teaches in its doctrine but using them for the powers that they embody in themselves. These are considered to have power of their own independent of what the doctrine teaches. Therefore, it is not a question of doctrine but power, belief and use or reasons of teleology.

Holy Water

It is a common religious experience for people to request for holy water blessed by a man of God and use it in many different ways. Holy water today is used in cooking to protect food from contamination with evil spirits. On some occasions, it is used in bathing or for protection against evil.

It is used by those who are sick to get well and some use it literary as medicine for curing physical ailments. In late 90s and 20s with the rise of the notion and fear of Satanism, the use of holy water became very popular and promoted by religious leaders.

In some Christian churches, holy water has a price on it. People would pay for holy water from men of God.

African traditional religions originally had no concept and use of water as baptismal water or holy water as practiced in Christianity. African traditional religions conceive water as having a spiritual force of its own and widely used as an agent in purification, cleansing and healing rites. It is used in the recovery of vital force. Water in some rites of cleansing, purification and healing is strengthened by adding certain ingredients of natural herbs or materials for efficacy and power.[215]

In African traditional religions water has been used in blessing of people, but in totally different ways from Christian traditions. Among the Babemba people of Northern Zambia an elderly person may hold water in the mouth, thrush the water with some inner force on the chest of person accompanied with incantations of blessings.

It is used to bless and sometimes mixed with kaolin for good tidings, respect, honour, and symbol of triumph and in initiations for some people on special occasions. Therefore, water in African traditions has a symbolism of life and blessing. Among Catholic Church members today at nearly every service, containers of litres of water are blessed every week for people to use. People are using this blessed water in many different ways, some not approved by the Catholic Church authority.

Even those who do not practice the Catholic faith are interested in this holy water. Holy water has been domesticated as one of those symbolic African traditional sacred materials with animated power and influence. The same applies to "anointing oil".

Anointing oil

Oil extracted from different natural plants, like palm blended with other healing mixtures is used as medicinal in some African

---

[215] Laurent Mpongo, "Contemporary African celebration of the Blessing of the Baptismal water in Roman Rite", *Concilium*, 178, 2, (1985), 62-69.

traditional societies, especially in Sub-Saharan Africa. Anointing oil is another religious material used in many different ways. People buy olive oils from shops take it to a man of God for blessing and people use it in their own ways and not what the Christian church teaches about it in accordance with doctrines.

Anointing oil has become so popular that it fetches some price from men of God. Sometimes it is packaged and sold for money. Anointing oil is used in some situations by people without being introduced to any instructions on Christian teachings.

People use it out of their natural belief and the power this oil contain. They believe it brings about healing of diseases, strength, protection against harm, good luck and many other ways only known by those who need and use it. In some way there is a shift from Christian traditional belief on the use of oil and bringing in an element of African traditional belief. This oil is now popular not only among Christian believers, even by those who do not belong to any denomination.

Christian Sacred Instruments

Christian ornaments like crosses and Catholic rosaries which are worn around necks and wrists are not just used for prayers but they are considered as powerful religious instruments to fend off evil and bringing about good tidings for people who use them.

Randomly asking some people with rosaries around their necks if they know how to pray the rosary as taught by the Catholic Church, many do not know, some are not even practicing and schooled in the Catholic faith. Many only know that there is power in moving around with a rosary around the neck or the wrist, bag or pocket.

All these are turned into religious symbols of power against evil and for good luck. All these materials after being blessed by a man of God become animated with religious and spiritual powers for protection, bringing fortunes, good health and healing purposes.

All these religious materials are used not only by those who believe in Christian faith, but even by people not schooled in the Christian faith and by people a Western missionary would consider to be pagans. Such uses of these religious materials are not bound by denomination but across denominations and non-practicing Christian.

By wearing them one feels protected from spiritual and physical harm. In some Christian churches some of these symbols carry no special doctrine along with them apart from what can be justified through the scriptures like the cross and anointing oil. Some of these have become like fetishes. This can be argued and considered as domestication of the concept of fetishism.

It is fetishism drawing its logic from African traditional religions which believes in certain materials as embodiments of supernatural powers. These, in some way, can connect people to the mystical world. Manufacturing of rosaries, Christian ornaments, statues and other Christian symbols have become big businesses by China, a country in which many of its people are not even practicing Christians.

Some Christian homes have created private household shrines with crosses, rosaries, statutes and sacred pictures. Domestic and house-hold shrines are a very important aspect of African traditional religions for offering prayers, veneration or worship and sacrifices. They are spaces of special prominence.

6.2 Priests, Pastors, Apostles, Prophets and Men of God

Today in most African countries, priests, pastors, apostles, prophets and men of God are playing out multiple roles in their communities. They are playing the roles of psychologists, counsellors, mediumistic figures, life and dream interpreters. Many do play these roles without any form of preparation in formal psychology and sociology.

They are using God-given gifts, inspirations, community belief and natural human understanding to get into the minds of clients, just as traditional healers do.

Very few traditional healers have attended formal studies in psychology, but they play it out with conviction and people believe in them, and there is no need to have a practicing licence like in the West. The community social approval certifies the roles of these people.

Priests, pastors, apostles, prophets and men of God are playing the role of economists, leading people into prosperity through prosperity gospel. Many have become good capitalists when it comes to "wealth creation" in the life of people through prayers.

Their followers can do anything they are told to do for them to prosper in their lives. The principles of "the more you give to God, the more you receive" and "the sowing of the seed of wealth" are never questioned. If things do not work, they are told to believe more for it is their lack of faith working against them.

Some priests, pastors, apostle, prophets and men of God have become full time politicians and at the same time, playing their religious roles and running churches. In Zambia, we have had religious-politicians in the sense that they are both leaders in religion and politics.

Some have been running government ministries, political parties and have reserved places at the pulpits. These are not fundamental issues for Zambians in combining the roles because they are part of the African world-view and the role of a religious leader. The separation of state and church is a Western premise. It does not exist in African world view.

Then priests, pastors, apostles, prophets and men of God play the role of intermediaries or the go-between, the invisible and the visible worlds. They have the capacity to oscillate between the two worlds as spiritual specialists. They are able to "see", "hear", "smell', "touch" and "taste" what ordinary people are not able to.

They are people with extraordinary senses of higher degree and level. They are like traditional hunters who can detect the trail of a hunted animal and in similar ways, priests, pastors, apostles, prophets and men of God have a spiritual capacity to trail and hunt down evil, misfortunes, sicknesses and other social challenges.

They are able to follow the trails or the foot-prints of the negative spirit that hold a person captive. Actually, this principle applies to traditional healers, diviners and witch finders as well in African traditional religions.

Some priests, pastors, apostles, prophets and men of God claim to have this gift of trailing negative sources of some spirit beings in people's lives. They can do this through prayers of exorcism, visions, telepathy, inspirations from God, prophetic messages and dreams.

They also play the role of healers, not only as spiritual healers, but physical healers as well and some are able to perform divination by trailing the origin of sources of failures, illnesses, misfortunes and social ills.

They have the power to deal with demons and evil spirits of, lack of marriage, barrenness, Satanism, bad luck, impotence and infertility, ancestral bondages, adultery, pre-marital sex, addictions like alcoholism and drugs, common family divorces, sexual intercourse with strangers and spirits of the under-world, among others, in the lives of people.

Some of these demons like the traditional ones may have their origin from under- world, under the seas, mountains, under-world demons, natural and spirits of the dead that come to haunt the- living. Some can even now claim to heal diseases that, in medical practice, are considered as life conditions like HIV, epilepsy, paralysis using the power of God.

Priests, pastors, apostles, prophets and men of God as ritual specialists have their authority, which lie in the fact of the intrinsic importance of rituals as instruments of mediating the relations between humans and non-human powers, invisible and visible, the known and the unknown.[216]

6.3. Religious Predations in Africa

It is difficult to isolate religion from the different realms of life in Africa. Religion has a strong relationship with politics and social life, economics, health and wealth. To a great extent, religion dictates general life of African people. This makes religion in Africa to have both positive and negative influence on life of many Africans.

This way of African people seeing a spiritual dimension to every important aspects of life makes Africans very unique in their religious spirituality. An African is able to identify the self with what is created and the whole of environment. This is one of the positive and unique aspects of African traditional religions which the early missionaries overlooked to exploit in the evangelization of Africans – sense of religiosity and deep spirituality.

An African has had a special relationship with the environment and the whole of creation. An African is born in this special relationship with the universe. An African already knows the impact of the negative relationship with creation, physical environment and the human space. African spirituality emphasizes a spiritual relationship with the surrounding and creation than just a resource for exploitation.

This African spirituality has been relegated from the heart, mind and life of an African by the European Christianity biased towards

---

[216] Cathrine Bell, Ritual Theory Ritual Practice (Oxford: Oxford University Press, 1992), 134.

capitalism. The Western mind has now come back as an expert to make an African aware of the importance of environment to human life.

Environmental spirituality or Eco-spirituality has always been part of African spirituality and life which has now been polluted by Western capitalism and Christianity. The belief of an African in the presence of supreme- being in creation was termed as animism by the Western theologian and sociological intellectuals. The complex African religion was reduced to animism. The European theologian took too quickly the symbolisms of African religions for an end in themselves. The world beyond of an African was relegated to the periphery. The practical spirituality of an African was considered as pagan and was suppressed and discarded all together.

The dictation of African spirituality, beliefs and their permeation of different realms of African life, has to be acknowledged that it leaves room for manipulations, abuse and predatory tendencies by those with religious authority and power.

An African religious leader holds a position of mediation between persons and other areas of life as lived in the present. A religious leader is believed to reconnect a person to prosperity, fruitfulness, productivity, successful leadership among people, good health and luck, and general success in life. The indispensability of African spirituality makes African religious leaders to hold a special place in the life of Africans.

They are respected as special people with special powers over the life of their followers. Many people today, for example in Zambia, have become so dependent on their pastors or men of God for their spiritual life, wealth creations, health maintenance and daily life.

These who are dependent on the "men of God" can do anything for these men of God because of the strong belief in them and their supernatural powers. Men of God are seen as figures that can influence God over the lives of their followers. Religious leaders because of this powerful and position of authority given to them by society, take advantage and make themselves into religious predators taking advantage of the strong religious belief of the people.

Predatory leadership, it has to be mentioned, is found in all spheres and levels of society. Predatory leadership can be found in street gangs, domestic violence, terrorist groups, schools and higher institutions of learning, political parties, both public and private business institutions, community social workers, among others.

Predatory tendencies in religion refer to the unethical strategies used and employed to use religious beliefs to take advantage of the people. [217] However, it has to be understood that people are manipulated, abused and taken advantage of not because people are irrational.

Religious leaders have taken advantage of the strong ingrained religious beliefs of an African in African traditional religions. Religious beliefs are turned into a business and wealth creation activity by men of God. Men of God can even sale anointed oils, spiritual shoes, T-shirts, holy water, under wears, Covid 19 (Coronavirus) masks and sanitizers, finger rings and many other items in the name of God.

People are encouraged to use these items in return for some blessings from God. Some women, both single and married are manipulated into having sexual encounters with some of the men of God to receive special blessings from God.

Some religious leaders have swindled their followers out of a lot of money, properties such as land, houses, household goods, among others. In the name of receiving special blessings from God through men of God, some people's monthly salaries, profits from their businesses go straight in the pockets of men of God. They are taught that the more they give to God, through the men of God, the more they are blessed.

The word of the man of God is a word of authority and power from God because one is anointed by God. This word of the man of God should never be contradicted or disregarded. Disregarding or speaking ill about the man of God is calling of a curse on oneself.

Predatory religious leaders take advantage of this and do not disclose amount of money received and collected, but the same leaders request their members to give records of finances, profits they make in their businesses, how much is their monthly salaries to calculate their tithe they are supposed to give regularly.

These religious leaders are free spenders without any scrutiny from anyone. These religious leaders are taken for granted as standing in for God who is just and fair. Followers of these religious leaders forget what the late former Zambian Republican president, Kenneth Kaunda, mentions about the reality of a human being.

---

[217] Neil Carter, The Predatory Side of Religion, Patheos.Com, Accessed on 09.05.2020.

Kaunda argues that in every human being there is an element of an animal that works towards destruction, selfishness, pride, manipulation of others, injustice, violence, abusing others and taking advantage of the weak. Kaunda continues to suggest that this reality calls for controls over this animal element in the human being.[218] This element is not taken away by being anointed by God. God anoints human beings and they serve as human beings as religious leaders. What can prevent this animal element in religious leaders not to take advantage of their followers?

Some of the religious leaders today use natural power and forces for selfish ideals. In African belief system, there is abundance of natural forces which can be exploited either for positive and negative motives.

And in some cases, scientific and critical mind is not applied, instead it is over shadowed and relegated to the fringes of objectivity and analysis. Instead, there is creation of fear of demons and God as punishing people for luck of faith. In this way, religion becomes a means of controlling the mind of the individuals through domination and subjugation.

Cultural and traditional authorities given to religious leaders make these leaders of religion to prey upon religious beliefs. This creates lies that are actually against some of the beliefs of genuine religion and creating unethical actions based on indirect coercive methods. Religion in this case becomes not a spiritual life-giving undertaking but a plague.[219]

Predatory religion sees disorder in human space and life as sign of the need to come back to the faith. Loss of job, failure to get married, some unexplained accidents and deaths, persistent illness, lack of success in business, inability to have children, anti-religious tendencies, mental and emotional breakdowns, abnormal sexual behaviour, sex with spirits and many other misfortunes, are sometimes interpreted as some signs of ancestral bondage and curses, loss of faith in God and making one vulnerable to demons and satanic forces.

For one to have control over life once again and normalize life, one needs help from men of God. It is at this point of vulnerability

---

[218] Kenneth Kaunda, Letter to my Children (London: Veritas, 1977), 130 - 132.

[219] Nicholas Shaw, The players of Religion (Aylesbury, Buckinghamshire, HP 22 5RR: Shield Crest, 2009).

of some people that some predatory religious tendencies by religious leaders are applied contrary to the genuine religion. Religion in this case is able to sniff out pain, loss, lack from afar and descends upon the suffering at their weakest point. This is predatory behaviour.

Predatory religious tendencies may include sexual abuses and exploitation in the disguise of belief to make way for marriage and ability to have children. Fraud, swindling in the name of reaching out to prosperity and other "irrational" acts like eating of grass, drinking of detergents and petrol for spiritual cleansing, waving of under wears in the air during prayer services for blessings of fertility, coming to religious services without under wears, being climbed on by religious leaders like on a horse riding, unaccounted for tithing and touching and anointing of sexual parts of human bodies in private prayers may all be interpreted as predatory tendencies.

Some religious leaders change their religious titles from pastors to "Papa". This creates a symbolic relationship of authority and submission between the religious leader and the followers. The title carries with it a connotation of a "provider, caregiver, loving figure, protector, guider" of his "children". This has a life-long psychological impact on the followers as long as they are under "Papa".

This relationship is transformed and used for predatory orientations. Papa relates in such way that he controls the lives of his little children in many aspects of human life. Some take the title of "Prophets" or "Apostle" for the same reasons. A prophet or an apostle of God cannot be questioned on his actions and demands. Questioning of a prophet or an apostle of God may invite a spiritual curse and misfortunes on a person.

Working against a prophet of God is working against God Himself. The religious leader is the only one who can hear God on behalf of the members in their personal situation.

6.4. Control of Predation in Religion in Africa

Today we have more voices calling for the control of religion because of the elements of predatory found in religious institutions. It has to be pointed out that we have lived in religious predatory environments for a long time. Some of the Western traditional religious institutions are calling for reformation of these institutions by opening them up to public scrutiny.

The question is, can these traditional Christian Churches reform themselves with such conservative foundation and traditions? This is yet to be seen and experienced with time. Over the years, religion has shown to have some elements of predatory tendencies that need attention to protect followers of religion.

Predation is not only found in the Christian religious traditional institutions. Predation is in nearly all religious institutions, what differs is the degree and openness to scrutiny and accountability to its followers and members. Members and followers in religions who call for accountability from their religious leaders are very few and at the same time, belief systems themselves do not give room for accountability. Asking for accountability from a man of God is like asking God to account to a human being. A human being and all he has, are gifts from God and the human being just takes a bit to give back to God and you ask God to account for that! This lack of accountability can be a source of fraud, manipulation and abuse of followers by religious leaders because they know that they are not accountable to anyone except to God.

This is an ideal when it comes to human beings. With human tendency to manipulate, exploit, seeking self-aggrandizement, self-pleasure and personal interests, the call for definable accountability is imperative even in religious experiences.

Some of the richest people in Africa today are among "men of God". Some own fleets of very expensive vehicles, private jets, exclusively expensive houses and designer shoes and suits. They take their children to very expensive schools where people who give offerings and tithe to them cannot afford to send their children.

They put on the most expensive and beautiful clothes which most of their followers cannot afford. Through this way, they indicate to their followers what faith in God can do in the life of those who are faithful to him. They present themselves as symbols of faithfulness, prosperity and success in God.

Their prosperity seen on their bodies and life are a symbol of reward from God for giving more to God and belief. These church leaders can lead their members to the same prosperity and success by following their instructions and guidance. Persistence of poverty is a sign of failure in faith in God on the part of a person.

With the strong African world-view or cosmology and religious belief systems influencing all areas of human life with strong belief in the power and authority of religious leaders from the background of traditional religions, is it possible that religious leaders can see the boundaries of respect in order to avoid abuse of religion for self-enrichment?

The question today is, should the governments or states in Africa come in to regulate religious institutions, experiences and making them a bit more "rational" and accountable to their followers? Or just who should make church leaders in Africa and Zambia in particular, accountable to their followers? The churches themselves or the governments? What cannot be put aside is the fact that, we are seeing more and more abuses, manipulations, fraud and white collar thieving in churches today, than ever before.

The other fact that cannot be over-looked is that religion in Zambia has become a very lucrative business and industry. Advertisements about churches and their pastors, prophets, apostles and their wives are found all over on streets and main highways on huge billboards at strategic points like traffic lights, round-abouts, road junctions and what is on offer during their services. Competition has become very high among the churches.

The only difference with other businesses and industries is that it is self-regulated and accountable to itself in terms of funds, healings, collection of tithe, morality and miracles and doctrines. A church is only found wanting when it breaks the law of the state.

Some of these churches have no definable regulations, rules and norms from a religious point of view which can protect their followers and members. This has been compounded in the case of Zambia with allowing the proliferation of churches under the banner of "Zambia being a Christian Nation".

Bus stations, marketplaces and schools have become places of evangelization including buses. Anything resembling Christianity is allowed to thrive in Zambia in the name of "Christian Nation". There is no serious or critical background checks on church leadership and their education background in matters of faith and Christian doctrine. One can register the existence of a church with the government without difficulties.

The predatory situation in which societies have found themselves with regard to religion, there is now a voice of advocacy for government regulation of existence of churches so that the government can have a hand on churches to protect the credulous members of society.

Some churches have rejected this position arguing on the basis of separation of church and state. Proponents of this position argue that belief is a question of human conscience and freedoms and it cannot be regulated by the state. The church argues from the point of view of respect, human protection from abuse and freedom of human conscience to believe in some supreme being.

Kyambalesa argues that the state should not be involved in religious issues. If anything, Zambia as a "secular state"[220] should just be silent about religion, not even to mention anything related to religion in the Constitution. Kyambalesa advocates a clear separation between the state and religion to safeguard each and every individual's freedom of worship and freedom to choose one's religion.

He proposes a need to introduce laws that are designed to keep religion out of politics and vice-versa.[221] At the same time, the rule of God cannot be brought under human authority. Therefore, separation between the state and the church is seen as the ideal relationship, though in some cases, this is just fictional separation which does not exist, especially in Africa, from the point of African traditional religions.

At the same time, some churches have no understanding of this separation between the state and the church. Some church leaders become part of the political establishment by becoming political leaders with positions in government or state machinery. In this case, even if the churches are not regulated by the government, they are somehow controlled in some ways through the governments" long underhand.

Government lack of regulation of religion, especially with regard to establishment of the churches in some respect is to the advantage of the political establishment. The more churches come into

---

[220] Kyambalesa by the terms "secular state" defines it as nation or a country that purports to be officially neutral in matters of religion, supporting neither religion nor irreligion. It is a state without an official religion. Therefore, Kyambalesa does not support the declaration, "Zambia as a Christian Nation". This is drawing religion into politics and politics into religion. While Kyambalesa suggests a complete separation between the state and religion, it has to be understood that in African way of life these two cannot be separated. This has made it very difficult for many people in Africa to see how possible this separation can be realized.

[221] Henry Kyambalesa, "Zambia: Religion, Politics and the State", https://www.lusakatimes.com. Accessed on 12.05.2020.

existence, the more of the voice of the church is polarized and diminished in talking about maladministration of the state.

It has to be pointed out that since the late 50s until the declaration of Zambia as a Christian Nation; the church had a strong voice in pointing out failures of the state in Zambia. Even the fighting for reintroduction of multiparty system of governance in 1991 in Zambia was partly a contribution from the voice of the Christian churches in Zambia speaking one strong critical voice about Kaunda's one party state or rule.[222]

The late president Fredrick Titus Jacob Chiluba was very much conscious of the strong voice of the church. Declaration of Zambia as a Christian Nation by Chiluba led to the proliferation of churches led by both indigenous Zambians and people of different nationalities.

Today, Zambia is a home to international Christian Churches from countries like Nigeria, Ghana, America, and other countries. Such proliferations of churches have led to weakening of the critical voice of the church about the misrule by the state.

This has worked to the advantage of the government in power. The voice of the Christian church has become very weak in spite that Zambia has had more churches than before 1991.

The political establishment thrives on different and dissenting voices among Christian churches to push for its own agenda. The late president Chiluba played the same political game on the unions for workers in the name of free speech but weakening the voice of the workers.

The more unions you have, the more you weaken the voice of the workers. This is the case as well, on the famous and infamous contentious Bill 10 about the national Constitution. The church is divided. Some are in support and some are against Bill 10.

Therefore, guidance of the church becomes polarized. Some churches have no understanding on the separation between religion and state in their theology. Today we have "men of God" and Pastors serving in government positions while still remaining religious leaders in their churches. Are these leaders advancing the agenda of the

---

[222] Pastoral Statement of the Catholic Bishops of Zambia, "Economics, Politics and Justice", Joe Komakoma (Edt), The Social Teaching of the Catholic Bishops and Other Christian Leaders in Zambia (Ndola: Mission Press, 2003), 224 – 236.

church or the state? Are these leaders conscious of the separation between the state and religion?

By presenting the above religious space, it has to be pointed out that it is difficult to find a fine line.

Predatory leadership in society can be brought under control when the majority of the people, including young people, are able to understand the fundamental premises of predatory religious leadership in relation to fundamental human rights.

In this way the society will be able to make better decisions about whom to follow, promote and elect to curb corruption, poverty and other social vices. It has to be understood that predatory leaders are not constrained by ethics and integrity. The predatory religious leaders usually lack capacity for empathy, ethics and conscience.[223]

---

[223] IMPADA Forum, "The solution to Predatory Leadership", http://predatoryleaders.com/wp-pl. Accessed on 12 December, 2019. IMPADA is a Non-Governmental Organization that stands for, International Movement for Peace and Dignity for All.

Conclusion

It is a fact that religion has power and authority of its own in society over human way of life, attitudes and way of looking at the world. This is true for every religion including African traditional religions. Sometimes there has been an underestimation of the power and influence of African traditional religions on Christianity.

Some scholars even predicted the end of influence of African traditional religions. There has always been a belief that when Africans understand the new religion brought to them in the name of Christianity, African traditional beliefs will just fall away and they will be no more. This has not been the case! African traditional religions still play a big role in the context of the new and "civilized" religions.

Of course, it has to be pointed out that the expression of African traditional religions takes into account the new context and social environment. In the past they used to talk about the existence of Christianity side by side with African traditional religions.

Today it is different. African traditional beliefs have become part of Christian expressions and practices. Pastors have become the embodiments of African traditional religions in subtle ways. Some pastors have taken over the role of African traditional religious leader, of a diviner, seer, prophet and a chief. These new religious leaders have used the authority, influence and power of an African traditional religious leader to their own advantage.

While these new religious leaders continue to demean some aspects of African traditional religions, at the same time they are riding on the very principles of these religions.

The new religious leader has tapped into African traditional religions and beliefs and expressing these beliefs in the context of new capitalistic environment. The new religious leader is very much aware of African traditional psychology, belief systems and logic of practice which find their basis in African world-view or cosmology. The new religious leader has exploited well the African logic of mystical interrelation of different realms of politics, economics and social relations. The new religious leader has taken the role of connecting these realms to the people. A religious leader has a role to play in socio-political, human body well-being and economics.

A religious leader is believed to connect people to prosperity and has power and authority to heal estranged relations that express themselves in form of illnesses and misfortunes. In this case illness is not only physical but it is spiritual as well.

The same applies to economic status and well-being of a person. The economic status of a person indicates one's standing in faith in God. This logic is informed by the African world-view which connects mystical powers to African fundamentals of life.

An African has continued to be an African traditional religious person in spite of embracing the new religion, which may be Christianity, Islam or any other religions.

This makes African traditional religion not as a stand-alone realm. Traditional African religious beliefs permeate nearly all areas of life of an African from birth to death and even including life after death. Actually, religion ties and connects every aspect of life to the other. This is makes a ritual to play an important role in everyday life of an African.

A ritual becomes a mystical instrument for connecting with the invisible world. A ritual connects an African with the source of life and origin of everyday well-being of an individual and society. It is this that gives a religious leader authority and power over the followers.

This authority of a religious leader being mystical falls outside critique, scrutiny and accountability to the followers. A religious leader in this case is "feared" and highly respected to be challenged. A religious leader can even make irrational and abusive demands on their followers in the name of religion because of this belief in their mystical power and authority.

Religion has enjoyed this uncontrolled power and authority for a long time, be it in traditional world religions or African traditional religions. It is a fact that religion has abused its power and authority in the name of belief. It is this belief in the power and authority of religious leaders which is the source of manipulation, abuse, fraud, mismanagement of resources of their churches. Such a scenario has given way to predatory religion. Religion sometimes feeds on vulnerable members of society. Some people have become "victims of religion" today. Many church leaders are collecting huge sums of money in the name of religion to which they are unaccountable to the people and donors. This is an element of predatory religion.

Religion in some way has been corrupted, abused and manipulated to a greater degree. Religion has become another industry in capitalistic society which exploits people for profit. The above makes the call for responsibility and accountability in religion a reasonable voice.

Religion should not continue operating in the mode of business as usual as it operated in the past. Religion needs to wake up to the new demands of society of taking responsibility and being accountable to the scrutiny of society.

On the debate of whether religion should regulate itself or be regulated by governments, the question is how does religion in the case of Zambia regulate itself, if it has to do this?

If it has to be exposed to government regulation to avoid abuse and manipulations, where is the line going to be drawn between the separation of religion and the state? While there should be separation between the state and religion there is an urgent call for protection of citizens from predators in religion from their abuses, corruption, fraud and manipulations.

It is a fact that religion in its history has been abusive of financial resources, human beings, especially the vulnerable, women and children. Religion has involved itself in fraud while riding on its unquestioned religious authority and power. Church institutions are partly human and divine institutions.

Society cannot let the human part of religion continue to reign and turning believers into "victims of religion". This is unacceptable! At the same time, followers in religions have to understand that religious leaders are humans as well.

They can be abusive, manipulative and exploitative. Followers in religion have to be alert and critical about certain demands made by their religious leaders in the name of faith and belief. It is a fact that predatory leaders are found in all human institutions without exception, schools, colleges, universities, workplaces, churches, hospitals, armies, police, political parties, among others.

Bibliography

Alberto, Moravia. Which tribe do you belong to? St. Albans, 1976.

Alt, Jennifer and Munro, Alison. Ubuntu-living: Being positive about people. Johannesburg: Catholic Psychological Services, 1997.

Ames, Michael. "Buddha and the Dancing Goblins: A theory of magic and religion". American Anthropologist, 66, 1964.

An Encyclopedia. Taylor and Francis Press, 2004.

Arthur, Lehman and Myers, James, eds. The Anthropological study of Religion, Magic, Witchcraft and Religion: An Anthropological study of Supernatural (2nd Edit). Mountain View: CA, Mayfield Publishing Company, 1989.

Baule, V. Susan. African Art in western Eyes. New Haven: Yale University Press, 1997.

Barnes, Sandra. "Ritual, Power and Outside Knowledge". Journal of Religion in Africa, XX, (3), 1990, 248 – 268.

Bayart, Jean-François, Ellis, Stephen and Hibou, Beatrice. The Criminalization of the state in Africa. Oxford: James Currey, 1999.

Beattie, John. Other Cultures: Aims, Methods and Achievements in Social Anthropology. London: Routledge, 1964.

Bediako Kwame. Christianity in Africa: The Renewal of a Non-Western Religion. Edinburgh: Edinburgh University Press, and Maryknoll, N.Y.: Orbis, 1995.

Behrend, Hike and Luig, eds. Spirit possession: Modernity and Power in Africa. Oxford: James Currey, 1999.

Bell, Cathrine. Ritual theory, Ritual Practice. Oxford: Oxford University Press, 1996.

Beller, Remy. Life, Person and Community in Africa. Limuru: Pauline Publication, 2001.

Bloch, Maurice. Ritual, History and Power: Selected papers in Social Anthropology. London: The Athlone Press, 1989.

Bourdieu, Pierre. Outline of a Theory of Practice. Cambridge and New York: Cambridge University Press, 1977.

Boyer, Pascal. The Naturalness of Religious Ideas: A cognitive Theory of Religion. Berkeley: University of California Press, 1994.

Bujo, Benezet. African Theology: In its Social Context. Nairobi: Don Bosco Training Centre Printing Press, 2003.

Broadbent, Samuel. A Narrative of the First Introduction of Christianity amongst the Barolong tribe of Bechuanas, South Africa with a brief summary of the subsequent history of the Wesleyan Mission to the same people. London: Wesleyan Mission House, 1865.

Burkert, Walter. The Creation of the Sacred: Tracks of Biology in early religions. Cambridge: Mass, 1996.

Carrithers, Michael. Why Humans have Cultures: Explaining Anthropology and Social Diversity. Oxford: Oxford University Press, 1992.

Carter, Neil. The Predatory Side of Religion, Patheos.Com.

Cassirer, Ernst. An Essay on Man: An Introduction to a Philosophy of Human Culture. Hamburg: F. Meiner, 2006.

Catechism of the Catholic Church,

Chipungu, N. Samuel. Guardians in their time: Experience of Zambians under Colonial rule, 1890 – 1964. London: The Macmillan Press Ltd, 1992.

Coetzee H., Preter and Roux P.J., Abraham. African Philosophy Reader. New York: Routledge, 1998.

Comaroff, Jean. Body of Power Spirit of Resistance. Chicago: The University of Chicago Press, 1985

Comaroff, John and Comaroff, Jean. Ethnography and Historical Imagination. Oxford: Westview Press, 1992.

Crehan, Kate. The Fractured community: Landscapes of Power and Gender in Rural Zambia. London: University of California Press, 1997.

Darwin, Charles. The Origin of Species. 6th Ed. London: John Murray, 1872.

Der B., G. "God and Sacrifices in the Traditional Religions of the Kasena and Dagaba of Northern Ghana". Journal of Religion in Africa, 11, 1980, 172 – 187.

Devisch, Rene. Weaving the threads of life. Chicago: Chicago University press, 1993.

Dillone – Malone, Clive. "The Mutumwa Church of Peter Mulenga – Part II". Journal of Religion in Africa, Vol. XVII, 1, 1987, 2 – 31.

Dondeyne, A. Foi Chretienne et pansee Contemporaine. Paris, 1961.

Downey, Michael, ed. The New Dictionary of Catholic Spirituality. Bagalore: Theological Publications in India, 1995.

Bart Duriez, Fontaine, R.J. Johnny and Hutsebaut, Dirk. "A further Elaboration of the Post-critical belief scale: Evidence for the Existence of Four Different Approaches to Religion in Flanders-Belgium", Psychologica Belgica, 40-3, 2000, 153-181.

Durkheim, Emile. Elementary forms of the Religious life, London: Hollen Press, 1915.

Eades J. S. The Yoruba Today. Cambridge: Cambridge University Press, 1980.

Ehset, Christopher. The Civilization of Africa: A history to 1800. Oxford: James Currey, 2002.

Ela, jean-Marc. My Faith as an African. New York: Orbis Books, 1988.

Ellis, Stephen and Garrie ter Haar. "Politics and African Religious Traditions". The Journal of Modern African Studies, Vol. 36, No. 2, June, 1998, 175 – 209.

Fabian, Johannes. Out of our Mind: Reason and Madness in the Exploration of Central Africa. London: University of California Press, 2000.

Fanon, Frantz. The Wretched of the Earth, Transl. Constance Farrington. New York: Grove Press, 1963.

Ferguson, James. Expectations of Modernity: Myths and Meanings of the Urban life on the Zambian Copperbelt. Los Angeles: University of California Press, 1999.

Fernandez W., James. "The Mission of Metaphor in Expressive Culture". Current Anthropology, 15, 2, 1974, 119 – 145.

_____."African Religious Movements". Annual Review of Anthropology, Vol. 7, 1978, 195 – 234.

Fisher J., Humphrey. "Conversion Reconsidered: Some Historical aspects of Religious Conversion in Black Africa". Africa, XLIII, 1, 1973, 27 – 40.

Frazer G., James. The Golden Bough: A New Abridgement. Oxford: Oxford University Press, 1994.

Freud, Sigmund. Totem and Taboo. London: George Routledge and Sons Ltd, 1919.

Frobenius, Leo, The Voice of Africa. Hutchison, Vol. 1, 1913.

Galgalo J. Joseph, African Christianity: The stranger within. Lumuru: Zapf Chancery Publishers Africa, 2012,

Gann, H., Lewis. The Birth of a Plural Society: The Development of Northern Rhodesia under the British South Africa Company 1894 – 1914. Manchester: Manchester University Press, 1958.

Geertz, Clifford. The Interpretation of Cultures. London: Fontana Press, 1973.

Glazier D., Stephen, ed. Anthropology of Religion. London: Praeger publishers, 1999.

Gledhill, John. Power and its Disguises: Anthropological Perspectives on Politics. London: Pluto Press, 1994.

Goody, Jack and Watt, Ian. "The Consequences of Literacy". Comparative Studies in Society and History, Vol. 5, No. 3, 1963.

Gordon, R. Lewis. Existential Africana. New York: Routledge, 2000.

Gramsci, Antonio. Prison Notebook. 1929 – 1935.

Grillo, S. Laura. "African Religions". Microsoft Encarta (DVD) premium, 2000, Redmond, 2008.

Guenther, Mathias. Tricksters and Trancers: Bushman Religion and Society. Bloomington: Indiana University Press, 1999.

Hahan, A. Robert. Sickness and Healing: Anthropological perspective. London: Yale University press, 1995.

Halls W. D. trans., "The Division of Labor in Society". New York: Simon and Schuster, 1997 (1897).

Hansen T. Karen, ed. African Encounters with Domesticity. New Jersey: Rutgess University Press, 1992.

Haring, Bernard. Medical Ethics Middlegreen: St. Paul Publications, 1991.

Harris, Marvin. Culture, People, Nature: An Introduction to General Anthropology 7th ed. New York: Longman, 1997.

Hess J. David. Science and Technology in Multicultural world. New York: Colombia University press, 1995.

Hill, Napoleon. The Law of Success. Mumbai: Magna Publishing Co. Ltd, 2010.

Hinfelaar, Hugo. "Bemba-speaking Women of Zambia in a Century of Religious Change (1832 – 1992)". Journal of Religion in Africa, Vol. 26, 2, 1994, 216 – 219.

Hodgson, Janet. "The Africanization of missionary Christianity: history and typology". Journal of Religion in Africa, Vol. XVI – 3, 1986, 187 – 208.

Hopkins M. Joseph. "Theological Students and Witchcraft Belief". Journal of Religion in Africa, Vol. XI, 1, 1980, 56 – 65.

Horton, Robin. "On the Rationality of Conversion". African Journal of the International African Institute, Vol. 45, 3, July 1975, 219 – 235 and Vol. 45, 4, October 1975, 373 – 399.

Huxley, Elspeth. The Sorcerers' Apprentice. London: Chatto and Windus, 1949.
Huxley, Thomas. Man's place in Nature and Other Essays. London: Macmillan, 1894.
Idow E. Bolaji. African Traditional Religions. London: S.C.M Press, 1973.
_____. Olodumare: God in Yoruba Belief. London: A & B Book Dist Inc, 1994.
Ingold, Tim, ed. Companion Encyclopedia of Anthropology: Humanity, Culture, and Social life. London: Routledge, 1994.
Izibili M. A. Enegho. "African Traditional Approach to the problems of Evil in the World". Stud Tribes Tribals, 7 (1), 2009, 11 – 15.
Kaniaki, D.D. and Evangelist Mukendi. Snatched from Satan's claws.
Kaunda, J. Chammah. 'The Nation That Fears God Prospers': A Critique of Zambian Pentecostal Theopolitical Imaginations. Philadelphia: Fortress, 2018.
_____. 'The Emptied Authority': African Neo-Pentecostalism, Modernization of Sacred Authority, And Gendered and Sexualized Constructions of Violence," Acta Theologica 40, no. 2, 2020.
Kaunda, Kenneth. Letter to my Children. London: Veritas, 1977.
Kelly D. John and Kaplan, Martha. "History, Structure and Ritual". Annual Review of Anthropology, Vol. 19, 1990.
Kertzer, David. Ritual, Politics and Power. London: Yale University Press, 1988.
Komakoma, Joe, ed. The Social Teaching of the Catholic Bishops and Other Christian Leaders in Zambia. Ndola: Mission Press, 2003.
Kyambalesa, Henry. Zambia: Religion, Politics and the State. https://www.lusakatimes.com.
Levi-Strauss, Claude. The Savage Mind. London: Weidenfeld and Nicolson, 1966.
Lossky, Nicholas, et al., eds. Dictionary of the Ecumenical Movement. Geneva: William B. Eerdmans Publishing Company, Grand Rapids, 1991.
Lubumbe, B. M. Bernard. Sunday Eucharistic Celebration: A critical Over-view. Ndola: Mission Press.
Lungu, F. Gatian, ed. Administrative Decentralization in Zambia Bureaucracy: An Analysis of Environmental Constraints. Lusaka: University of Zambia Institute for African Studies, No.18, 1985.

Mackey, D. j. "Simon Kimbangu and the B.M.S. tradition", Journal of Religion in Africa, Vol. XVII – 2, 1987,113 – 171.

Malinowski, Bronislaw "Anthropology". Encyclopedia Britannica, 1926.

_____. Sex, Culture and Myth. London: R. Hart-Davis, 1963.

Makau, Mutua. Human Rights: A Political and Cultural Critique. Philadelphia: University of Pennsylvania Press, 2002.

Marx, Karl and Engels, Fredrick. On Religion. Atlanta: Schochen Books, 1964.

Mazrui A. Ali. The African Condition: A political diagnosis. Cambridge: Cambridge University press, 1995.

Mbiti, S John. African Religions and Philosophy. London, Ibadan, Nairobi: Heinemann, 1969.

_____ Introduction to African Religion. Nairobi: East Africa Education Publishers Ltd., 1990.

Merton, Robert. "Social Structure and Anomie". American Sociological Review, Vol. 3, (5), 1938, 672 – 682.

Mildnerova, Katerina. "African Independent Churches in Zambia (Lusaka)", Ethnologia Actualis, Vol. 14, No. 2/2014.

Moravia, Alberto. Which tribe do you belong to? New York: Farrar, Straus and Giroux, 1976.

Mosley G. Albert. African Philosophy. New Jersey: Prentice Hall, 1995.

Mpong, Laurent. "Contemporary African celebration of the blessing of the baptismal water in Roman Rite". Concilium, 1985, 62 – 68.

Mugambi, Jesse. Critique of Christianity in African Literature. Nairobi: Heineman, 1992.

Muller, E. Klaus and Ritz-Muller, Ute. Soul of Africa: Magical Rites and Traditions. Maxeville: Konemann, 2000.

Mutale, Tresphor. Zambian Democracy betrayed: Patrimonial corruption in Zambia, Ndola: Mission Press, 2008.

Neckebrouck, Valeer. Anthropological Study of African Religion. (University lecture notes), University of Leuven, 2000.

Nkemnkia, N. Martin. African Vitality: A step forward in African Thinking. Limuru: Pauline Publication, 1999.

Nkrumah, Nkwame. Ghana: The Autobiography of Nkwame Nkrumah. Edinburgh: Nelson, 1957.

Novak, Michael. Belief and Unbelief: A Philosophy of Self-knowledge. New York and Toronto: The New American Library, 1965.

Nyamiti, Charles. African Tradition and the Christian God. Eldoret: Gaba Publications, Spearhead No. 49.

Nyangisa, J. Ooko. Healing your Family Tree. Limuru – Kenya: Franciscan Kolbe Press, 2010.

Ogot, B. A. Some Approaches to African History. Nairobi: Hadith, 1968.

Parrinder, Geoffrey. Witchcraft: European and African. London: Faber, 1963.

Parsons, Talcott. The Structure of Social Action. Glencoe: The Free Press, 1949.

Pobee, S. John. "Religion and Politics in Ghana, 1972 – 1978: Some case studies from the rule of General I.K. Acheampong", Journal of Religion in Africa, Vol. XVII, 1, 1982.

Pontificum Concilium de Cultura. Identifying Challenges and Priorities in a Pastoral Approach to Cultures in Africa: Handing on the Faith at the Heart of Africa's Culture. Vatican.

Pritchard, Evans. Theories of Primitive Religion. Oxford: Oxford University press, 1965.

Ray C. Benjamin. African Religions: Symbol, Ritual and Community. New Jersey: Prentice Hall, 2000.

Sapong, K. Peter. People Differ. Accra: Sub-Saharan Publishers, 2002.

Shaw Nicholas. The players of Religion, Aylesbury, Buckinghamshire, HP 22 5RR: Shield Crest, 2009.

Shank, A. David. "The Harrist church in the Ivory Coast" (Review Article), Journal of Religions in Africa, Vol. XV – 1, 1985, 67 – 75.

Smith E. William, ed. African Ideas of God. London: Edinburgh House Press, 1966.

Soltyk, Malgorzata. "Invoking Spirits", Love One Another, No. 47.

Sowell, Thomas. Conquest and Cultures: An International History. New York: Basic Books, 1998.

Spaulding, John, trans. "Suicide: A study in Sociology". New York: The Free Press, 1979 (1897).

Stumpf E. Samuel. Socrates to Sartre: A History of Philosophy. 3rd ed. New York: McGraw-Hill Book Company, 1982.

Tempels, Placid, ed. Bantu Philosophy. Paris: Presence Africaine, 1969.

Trinitapoli, Jenny and Weinreb, Alexander. Religion and AIDS in Africa. New York: Oxford University Press, 2012.

Turner, W. Harold. "The way forward in the Religious study of African Primal Religions", Journal of Religion in Africa, Vol. XII, 1, 1981.

Turner, Victor. The Forest of Symbols: Aspects of Ndembu Ritual. London: Cornell University Press, 1962.

Tutu M. Desmond. "Black Theology/African Theology - Soul Mates or Antagonists?" In A Reader in African Christian Theology. London: SPCK, 1987.

Tylor B. Edward. Researches into the Early History of Mankind and the Development of Civilization. 3rd ed. London: John Murray, 1878.

Udelhoven, Bernhard. Satanism in Zambia: Touched by the finger of Thomas (Notes for a Seminar), 2008.

Unknown Author. Nature Customs: A Study of the Babemba and Neighbouring Tribes.

Wariboko, Nimi. The Split God: Pentecostalism and Critical Theory. Albany, New York: State University of New York Press, 2018.

Weber, Max. The Protestant Ethic and the Spirit of Capitalism. London: George Allen and Unwin, 1904 – 1905.

Werbner, Richard and Ranger, Terence. Postcolonial Identities in Africa. New Jersey: Zed Books, 1996.

Wilson, Brayan, ed. Rationality. Oxford: Basil Blackwell, 1977.

Religion in Sociological Perspective. Oxford: Oxford University Press, 1982.

Wilson, Monica. Communal Ritual of the Nyakyusa. London: Routledge, 1959.

Zack-Williams, Tunde, Frost, Diane and Thomson, Alex, eds. Africa in Crisis: New Challenges and Possibilities. London: Pluto Press, 2002.

www.ingramcontent.com/pod-product-compliance
Lightning Source LLC
Chambersburg PA
CBHW050906300426
44111CB00010B/1408